Get Updates and More on Nolo.com

Go to this book's companion page at:

www.nolo.com/back-of-book/ARBNB.html

When there's an important change to the law affecting this book, we'll post updates. You'll also find articles and other related materials.

More Resources from Nolo.com

Legal Forms, Books, & Software
Hundreds of do-it-yourself products—all written in plain English, approved, and updated by our in-house legal editors.

Legal Articles
Get informed with thousands of free articles on everyday legal topics. Our articles are accurate, up to date, and reader friendly.

Find a Lawyer
Want to talk to a lawyer? Use Nolo to find a lawyer who can help you with your case.

NOLO
LAW for ALL

4th Edition

Every Airbnb
Host's Tax Guide

Stephen Fishman, J.D.

FOURTH EDITION	JANUARY 2021
Editor	DIANA FITZPATRICK
Book Design	SUSAN PUTNEY
Proofreading	IRENE BARNARD
Index	SONGBIRD INDEXING SERVICES
Printing	BANG PRINTING

Names: Fishman, Stephen, author.
Title: Every Airbnb host's tax guide / Stephen Fishman, J.D.
Other titles: Every Airbed-and-breakfast host's tax guide
Description: 4th edition. | Berkeley, California : Nolo, 2021. | Includes
   index.
Identifiers: LCCN 2020033208 (print) | LCCN 2020033209 (ebook) | ISBN
   9781413328202 (paperback) | ISBN 9781413328219 (ebook)
Subjects: LCSH: Bed and breakfast accommodations--Taxation--Law and
   legislation--United States. | Vacation rentals--Taxation--Law and
   legislation--United States. | Rental housing--Taxation--Law and
   legislation--United States.
Classification: LCC KF6495.H67 F57 2021 (print) | LCC KF6495.H67 (ebook)
   | DDC 343.7306/6--dc23
LC record available at https://lccn.loc.gov/2020033208
LC ebook record available at https://lccn.loc.gov/2020033209

This book covers only United States law, unless it specifically states otherwise.

Please note

We know that accurate, plain-English legal information can help you solve many of
your own legal problems. But this text is not a substitute for personalized advice from
a knowledgeable lawyer. If you want the help of a trained professional—and we'll
always point out situations in which we think that's a good idea—consult an attorney
licensed to practice in your state.

Acknowledgments

Many thanks to:

Diana Fitzpatrick for her outstanding editing

Susan Putney for book design

Irene Barnard for proofreading

Songbird Indexing Services for the index

About the Author

Stephen Fishman has dedicated his career as an attorney and author to writing useful, authoritative, and recognized guides on taxes and business law for small businesses, entrepreneurs, independent contractors, and freelancers. He is the author of over 20 books and hundreds of articles, and has been quoted in the *New York Times*, *Wall Street Journal*, *Chicago Tribune*, and many other publications. Among his books are *Every Landlord's Tax Deduction Guide; Deduct It! Lower Your Small Business Taxes; Working With Independent Contractors;* and *Working for Yourself: Law and Taxes for Independent Contractors, Freelancers & Gig Workers of All Types*. All are published by Nolo.

Table of Contents

Introduction: Who This Book Is For

This book—the first of its kind—is a guide to the income tax issues faced by people who rent out all or part of their homes to short-term guests. We refer to such people as short-term rental hosts. The information here applies to rentals arranged through online rental platforms, such as Airbnb, VRBO, FlipKey, and others. It also applies to short-term rentals made through Craigslist, or made offline through local advertising, word-of-mouth, or any other means.

This book provides the tax knowledge rental hosts need whether they rent out all or part of their main home, vacation home, or any other property they own or rent, like a cottage or separate unit attached to their home. The tax rules for short-term rental hosts are different from those that apply to traditional landlords. If you're a traditional landlord who rents property full time to long-term tenants (or if a short-term guest ends up being a long-term tenant), refer to *Every Landlord's Tax Deduction Guide*, by Stephen Fishman (Nolo), for in-depth guidance on all the tax issues you face.

Taxes are complicated enough for traditional landlords, but they can be even more difficult for short-term rental hosts. Online rental platforms provide little or no tax guidance—they're in the rental business, not the tax advice business. Many tax professionals have little understanding of the unique tax problems posed by short-term rentals. This book is intended to fill that void. It provides all the information short-term rental hosts need to minimize their taxes and stay out of trouble with the IRS, including:

- when short-term rentals are tax free
- how to identify, allocate, and maximize short-term rental deductions
- IRS reporting for short-term rentals
- how to deduct short-term rental losses

- completing your tax return (IRS Schedule E), and
- record keeping for short-term rentals.

Now more than ever you need guidance when it comes to taxes for your short-term rental activity. In 2017, Congress enacted the most sweeping changes to the tax code in over 30 years when it passed the Tax Cuts and Jobs Act (TCJA), which took effect in 2018. Now, in an effort to stave off economic devastation in the wake of the coronavirus (COVID-19) pandemic, Congress revised the nation's tax laws yet again, temporarily suspending many of the harshest provisions of the TCJA. We explain how all these changes affect hosts, including how you can use the new tax deduction for pass-through business owners to reduce the income taxes you pay on your rental income by up to 20%.

Even if you work with an accountant or other tax professional, you need to understand these tax issues. Doing so will help you provide your tax professional with better records, ask better questions, obtain better advice, and, just as importantly, evaluate the advice you get from tax professionals, websites, and other sources. If you do your taxes yourself, your need for knowledge is even greater. Not even the most sophisticated tax preparation software provides the insights and specialized guidance you'll find in this book.

Minimizing the taxes you pay on your rental income can make your hosting activity far more profitable—indeed, it can spell the difference between making and losing money. The time to start planning to reduce the taxes you'll need to pay on your short-term rental income is now. You can't wait until April 15—by then it will be too late to implement most of the tax savings strategies and procedures covered in this book.

Get Updates to This Book on Nolo.com

When there are important changes to the information in this book, we'll post updates online, on a page dedicated to this book:

www.nolo.com/back-of-book/ARBNB.html

How Short-Term Rental Hosts Are Taxed

This chapter explains the type of taxes short-term rental hosts need to know about:

- income taxes
- Social Security and Medicare taxes
- Net Investment Income tax, and
- local and state occupancy taxes.

Most short-term rental hosts have to pay income taxes and some have to pay Social Security and Medicare taxes as well. Although hosts don't have to pay local occupancy taxes themselves, they have to ensure that these taxes are paid by their guests.

Income Taxes

Short-term rental hosts must be concerned first and foremost with federal income taxes. If you rent your property for 14 days or less during the year, you may not have to pay any income tax at all on your rental income. This is discussed in detail in Chapter 3. However, if, like most short-term rental hosts, you rent your property more than 14 days, you'll have to pay federal income tax on the net rental income you receive during the year. When you file your yearly tax return, you add your net rental income to your other income for the year, such as salary income from a job, interest on savings, and investment income, and you pay income tax on the total. You'll need to file a separate tax form with your annual tax return (usually IRS Schedule E) to report your short-term rental income and expenses (see Chapter 10).

Fortunately, you need not pay tax on all the short-term rental income you receive. Instead, you pay tax only on your "net" rental income—this is your total rental income minus your deductible rental property expenses. Thus, the more deductible expenses you have, the less tax you'll have to pay.

EXAMPLE: Jackie owns a condo in Miami that she rents out 60 days during the year on Airbnb, earning a total of $6,000 in rental income. Luckily, she does not have to pay income tax on the entire $6,000. She gets to deduct the expenses she incurred renting out her condo, such as Airbnb fees, utilities, supplies, repairs, and depreciation of her condo. These amount to $2,000. She need only pay income tax on her $4,000 in net short-term rental income. She files IRS Schedule E with her tax return to report her rental income and expenses. She adds her $4,000 net short-term rental income to her other income for the year and pays income tax on the total.

This example shows why it is so important to deduct every rental expense you're allowed and to keep proper records of these deductions in case they are questioned by the IRS.

In some cases, your deductible expenses can exceed the income you earn from renting your property, resulting in a net rental loss for the year. Rental losses can be deductible from other nonrental income you earned during the year. The complex tax rules governing these kinds of losses are covered in Chapter 12.

State Income Taxes

This book covers federal taxes. However, 43 states also have income taxes. State income tax laws generally track federal tax law, but there are some exceptions. The states without income taxes are Alaska, Florida, Nevada, South Dakota, Texas, Washington, and Wyoming. For details on your state's income tax law, visit your state tax agency's website, or contact your local state tax office. You can find links to all 50 state tax agency websites at www.taxadmin.org/state-tax-agencies.

What Is Rental Income?

Your rental income consists primarily of the rent your short-term guests pay you for the use of your property. However, short-term rentals can generate other income as well. Here are examples of some other types of rental income.

Security deposits. You do not need to include security deposit money in your income when you receive it if you plan to return the money to your guests at the end of their stay. However, if you keep part or all of the security deposit because a guest causes damage or doesn't pay you in full at the end of their stay, include the amount you keep in your income for that year. If the guest caused damage, you can deduct the cost of repairs (see Chapter 4).

Interest earned on security deposits is also rental income that should be included in your income in the year it is earned, unless your state or local law requires landlords to credit that interest to your guests.

Property or services in lieu of rent. Property or services you receive from a guest as rent (instead of money) must be included in your rental income. For example, if a guest is a painter and offers to paint your property in return for staying rent free for 30 days, you must include in your rental income the amount the guest would have paid for a 30-day stay at your property.

Rental expenses paid for by guests. Any rental expenses paid for by guests are rental income; for example, payments a guest makes to you for repairs, utilities, or other rental costs. These costs are then deductible by you as rental expenses.

Reservation cancellation fees. Any fees you retain when a guest cancels a reservation are rental income.

Fees. Other fees or charges guests pay you are also rental income. These include:

- garage or other parking fees
- fees you charge guests for use of storage facilities
- pet fees, and
- laundry income from washers and dryers you provide for guests' use.

What Expenses Are Deductible?

You are entitled to deduct virtually all the expenses you incur when you rent out your property, just like any other residential landlord. This includes such items as advertising costs, attorneys' and accounting fees, listing fees and commissions, travel expenses, mortgage interest, utilities, supplies, travel expenses, car expenses, repairs and maintenance, furniture and personal property costs, and depreciation of your real property.

Any expenses you incur just for your short-term rental activity—for example, Airbnb listing fees—are fully deductible. However, other expenses are only partly deductible. Deductions such as depreciation and repairs must be prorated according to the amount of time you rent your property during the year compared with the time you use it personally; and, if you don't rent your entire property, by the amount of space that is rented. For example, if you rent your entire home 10% of the year, you'll be able to deduct only 10% of the depreciation you'd be able to claim for a full-time rental. If you have a room that takes up 25% of the space in your home and you rent the room for 10% of the year, you'd be entitled to 2.5% of the full depreciation deduction for the entire home. How to calculate the rental and personal use of your property, and how to allocate your deductions, is covered in detail in Chapter 9.

Paying Estimated Tax on Your Rental Profits

No income or other taxes are withheld from the rental payments you receive from online rental platforms like Airbnb and VRBO. Be aware, however, that when you set up your account with an online platform like Airbnb, VRBO, or FlipKey, you must provide a completed IRS W-9, *Request for Taxpayer Identification Number and Certification*. This verifies your identity and address for tax purposes. If you don't complete a W-9, the company is required to withhold 24% of your rental income and pay it to the IRS. This is called backup withholding.

If your short-term rental activity earns a profit and you expect to owe at least $1,000 in income tax on the amount, you may need to pay estimated taxes to the IRS to prepay your income tax liability. However, if you work and have income tax withheld from your pay, you'll need to pay estimated tax only if your total withholding (and any tax credits) amounts to less than 90% of the total tax you expect to pay for the year. Thus, you can avoid paying any estimated tax at all by having your withholding increased. But, you'll be able to hold on to your money a bit longer if you pay estimated tax instead of having the money taken out of your paychecks every pay period.

If you pay estimated tax, the payments are due four times per year: April 15, June 15, September 15, and January 15. To avoid having to pay an underpayment penalty, your total withholding and estimated tax payments must equal the lesser of either (1) 90% of your tax liability for the current year, or (2) 100% of what you paid the previous year (or 110% if you're a high-income taxpayer—adjusted gross income of more than $150,000; or $75,000 for married couples filing separate returns).

The easiest way to calculate your quarterly estimated tax payments is to subtract your total expected income tax withholding for the current year from the total income tax you paid last year. The balance is the total amount of estimated tax you must pay this year. But, if you're a high-income taxpayer, add 10% to the total. Note, however, that if your income is higher this year than last, you'll owe extra tax to the IRS on April 15. To avoid this, you can increase your estimated tax payments or simply save the money you'll need to pay the taxes when you file your annual return.

You pay the money directly to the IRS in four equal installments, so divide the total by four. You can pay by mail, electronic withdrawal from your bank account, or by credit or debit card. For details, see the IRS estimated tax webpage at www.irs.gov/Businesses/Small-Businesses-Self-Employed/Estimated-Taxes.

Income Taxes When You Sell Your Home

If you rent your main home on a short-term basis, there may be income tax consequences when you sell it.

Recapture of Depreciation

First of all, if you sell the home at a profit, you will be required to recapture all the depreciation deductions you took (or should have taken) during the years you rented the home. (See Chapter 7 for a detailed discussion of depreciation.)

You must report the total amount of depreciation on IRS Form 4797 and pay a flat 25% tax on it (however, if your top income tax rate is below 25%, the lower rate applies). This can have a significant tax impact. For example, if you rented your home part time through Airbnb for five years and took $10,000 in total depreciation deductions, you'll owe $2,500 in tax when you sell the home. If you separately depreciated personal property used in your rental activity, depreciation recapture is taxed at your ordinary income tax rates—as high as 37%.

Impact of Short-Term Rentals on Home Sale Tax Exclusion

Ordinarily, when you sell real property you must pay income tax (at capital gains rates) on any profit you earn from the sale. However, when you sell your main home you may qualify for a huge tax break: If you own and occupy the home as your principal residence for at least any two of the five years before you sell it you don't have to pay income tax on up to $250,000 of the gain from the sale if you're single, or up to $500,000 if you're married and file jointly. (But you must still pay the 25% tax on your depreciation recapture.) Your two years of ownership and use can occur anytime during the five years before you sell—and you don't have to be living in the home when you sell it.

For a home to be your principal residence, you must live in it a majority of the time during the year. Thus, if you rent out your home for over half the year, you can't count that year toward your two years of personal use. However, the IRS says that "short temporary absences for vacations or other seasonal absences, even if you rent out the property during the absences" still count as time you live in your home. The IRS provides no exact guidelines about how long such a temporary absence can be. However, according to IRS examples, a two-month absence during which your home is rented would count as short and temporary, but a one year absence would not. Thus, the short-term rental of your entire home for a total of a few months per year should not prevent you from qualifying for the home sale tax exclusion.

> EXAMPLE: David bought and moved into his home on February 1, 2019. Each year during 2019 and 2020, David left his home for a two month summer vacation and rented out the home through Airbnb. David sold the house on March 1, 2021. Although the total time David actually used his home is less than two years (21 months), he meets the requirements for the home sale exclusion. The two month vacations are short, temporary absences and are counted as periods of use in determining whether David used the home for the required two years.

However, rentals for a total of more than a few months could cause the IRS to view your home as ceasing to be your principal residence and jeopardize your exclusion if, as a result, you fail to meet the two-out-of-five-year rule. If you're in this situation, consult with a tax professional before you sell your home.

Additionally, if you convert a portion of your home into a separate rental unit (with its own entrance, kitchen, and bathroom), and sell your property more than three years later, you must treat the transaction as if there were two sales—one the sale of a residence, the other the sale of a rental property. You must allocate the sales price, expenses, and tax basis (cost) between the residence and rental parts. You can only apply the home sale exclusion toward the allocated profit you earned from selling the residence portion of the property. Moreover, you must adjust the rental part's basis downward to reflect the depreciation deductions you took, or should have taken. The same rule applies if you use a separate structure on your property, such as a guest house, for rental purposes. (IRS Reg. § 1.121-1(e)(4).)

For more details on the home sale tax exclusion, see IRS Publication 523, *Selling Your Home.*

Social Security and Medicare Taxes

As you doubtless know, people who work as employees or own their own businesses are required to pay Social Security and Medicare taxes on their income as well as income taxes, up to annual limits. Ordinarily, the money landlords earn from renting their property is not subject to Social Security and Medicare taxes. This rule applies to short-term rental hosts as well as to traditional residential landlords. (IRS Reg. § 1.1402(a)-4(c).) However, there is an important exception to this general rule: It does not apply to individuals who are running a hotel or bed and breakfast business. These are service businesses, not purely rental activities. They are classified as regular businesses for tax purposes and the profits earned from them are subject to Social Security and Medicare tax. Your short-term rental activity will be classified the same as a hotel or a bed and breakfast by the IRS if you provide your guests with substantial personal services—that is, personal services that are typically not provided by traditional landlords, such as cooking and maid services. Because your activity is classified as a regular business for tax purposes, not a rental activity, you report your income and expenses on IRS Schedule C, *Profit or Loss from Business*, not Schedule E. If you earn a profit from your activity, you'll not only have to pay income tax on your profit, but Social Security and Medicare taxes as well. One advantage of filing Schedule C is that it is easier to deduct losses. Schedule C filers may deduct all of their rental losses from nonrental income so long as they materially participate in the rental activity. In contrast, Schedule E filers who are not real estate professionals may only deduct $25,000 in annual losses, even if they materially participate—and even this limited deduction is unavailable to higher-income filers. (See Chapter 12.) Many short-term rental hosts provide their guests with substantial services without being aware how it affects their tax treatment.

What Are Substantial Services?

The services we're talking about are services other than those residential landlords renting their property on a long-term basis typically provide their tenants. Thus, they do not include utilities (water, electricity, heat, air-conditioning), trash collection, cleaning of public areas, or building repairs and maintenance. Rather, they are hotel-like services provided for guests' convenience, not to maintain the property. A good example is supplying daily maid service—this is a service provided by hotels and bed and breakfast businesses, not residential landlords. Other examples include providing:

- meals or snacks
- laundry services
- books, games, and videos
- concierge services
- tours and outings
- transportation
- amenities like linens, irons, hangers, shampoo, and soap, or
- other hotel-like services.

However, providing such services is not enough in itself to turn your rental activity into a hotel business. The services must be "substantial"— that is, their value must constitute a "material part of the payments made by the tenant." (IRS Rev. Rul. 1983-139.) The IRS provides no precise guidelines on exactly how much services must be worth to be substantial, but examples in IRS Regulations indicate they must be worth at least 10% to 15% of the total rent paid by the guests. (IRS Reg. §§ 1.1402(a)-4(c)(3), 1.469-1T(e)(3)(viii), Ex. 4.) Thus, for example, simply supplying your guests with towels and soap or a few other amenities of limited value would likely not rise to the level of "substantial services." On the other hand, if you provide daily meals and maid and laundry services to your guests, you could be providing substantial services.

Remember, this category applies both to those who rent out their entire homes and those who rent a room or rooms in their home (or apartment).

EXAMPLE: Jean-Claude has a four-bedroom home in the mountains. This year, one bedroom was rented to 30 different guests for 280 days and another bedroom to 50 guests for 330 days. He provides his guests with daily breakfasts and snacks, daily maid service, laundry service, skis and ski lessons, linens, and shampoo and other toiletries. He personally picks up and drops off many of his guests at the airport. He provides substantial services to his guests, so his rental activity qualifies as a hotel or bed and breakfast for tax purposes.

File IRS Schedule C

If your rental activity is treated as a hotel or bed and breakfast business, you report your income and expenses on IRS Schedule C, *Profit or Loss From Business*, not on Schedule E, the schedule used by residential landlords. Schedule C is used for all types of individually owned businesses. If you own your rental through a multimember LLC, corporation, or partnership, you file the appropriate return for that type of business entity (single-member LLC owners still file Schedule C).

Social Security and Medicare Tax Due on Rental Profits

When you have a Schedule C business, you must pay Social Security and Medicare on your profits (these are also called self-employment taxes). You file IRS Schedule SE with your return to report these taxes. You should include these taxes with the estimated tax payments you make each year.

Social Security tax. The Social Security tax is a flat 12.4% tax on net self-employment income up to an annual ceiling that is adjusted for inflation each year. In 2020, the ceiling was $137,700 in net self-employment income. Thus, if you have that much or more in net self-employment income, you would pay $17,075 in Social Security taxes.

Medicare tax. There are two Medicare tax rates: a 2.9% tax up to an annual ceiling—$200,000 for single taxpayers and $250,000 for married couples filing jointly. All income above the ceiling is taxed at a 3.8% rate. Thus, for example, a single taxpayer with $300,000 in net self-employment income would pay a 2.9% Medicare tax on the first $200,000 of income and a 3.8% tax on the remaining $100,000.

You pay these taxes only on your net self-employment income—that is, the profit you earn from your Schedule C business after deducting all your expenses. If you have more than one business, you combine your net income from all of them to determine your total self-employment income for the year. If you have an employee job, you and your employer each pay half of these Social Security and Medicare taxes on your wages in the form of payroll taxes that are withheld from your pay. If your wages exceed the annual Social Security tax limit, you won't have to pay any Social Security tax on your hotel business income (or any other self-employment income). But you must pay the Medicare tax on all your employee and self-employment income, no matter how high.

Net Investment Income Tax

In addition to regular income taxes, higher-income hosts may be subject to the Net Investment Income (NII) tax. The NII tax was enacted in 2010 to help fund the Affordable Care Act, popularly known as Obamacare.

What Is the NII Tax?

The NII tax is a separate 3.8% income tax on unearned income—that is, income other than from a job or business in which you actively participate. Those subject to it—primarily higher-income taxpayers—must pay it in addition to their regular income taxes. The tax is included on Form 1040. You report the amount you're required to pay by completing IRS Form 8960, *Net Investment Income Tax—Individuals, Estates, and Trusts*, and attaching it to your return.

Who Is Subject to the NII Tax?

You'll be subject to the NII tax only if your adjusted gross income (AGI) for the year exceeds $200,000 if you're single, or $250,000 if you're married filing jointly (the threshold is $125,000 for married couples filing separately). If you add up all of your income from every source, and the total is less than the applicable $200,000/$250,000 threshold, you will not be subject to this tax.

What Is Net Investment Income?

Even if your AGI exceeds the $200,000/$250,000 threshold, you'll be subject to the NII tax only if you have net investment income. Net investment income consists of:

- net rental income (rents minus expenses)
- income from investments, including interest, dividends, and annuities
- income from any business in which you don't materially participate, including real estate limited partnerships and other real estate investment businesses, and
- net capital gains (gains less capital losses) you earn upon the sale of property that is not part of an active business, including rental property, stocks and bonds, and mutual funds.

Amount of the Tax

The NII tax is a flat 3.8% tax that must paid on the *lesser* of (1) the taxpayer's net investment income, or (2) the amount that the taxpayer's AGI exceeds the applicable threshold. $200,000 for single taxpayers, and $250,000 for married filing jointly.

> EXAMPLE: Burt, a single taxpayer, has a job that pays him $300,000 in wages. He also earned $30,000 in net rental income from renting out his main home and vacation home part time on Airbnb. His rental income is net investment income subject to the NII tax. His

AGI is $330,000. Burt must pay the 3.8% NII tax on the lesser of (1) his $30,000 of net investment income, or (2) the amount his $330,000 AGI exceeds the $200,000 threshold for single taxpayers—$130,000. Since $30,000 is less than $130,000, he must pay the 3.8% tax on $30,000. His NII tax for the year is $1,140 (3.8% × $30,000 = $1,140).

Real Estate Professionals Not Subject to NII Tax

If you're a real estate professional, you're exempt from the NII tax if (1) you materially participate in your hosting activity, and (2) the activity qualifies as a business for tax purposes. See the discussion of real estate professionals and material participation in Chapter 12.

Hosts in Hotel Business Not Subject to NII Tax

Some hosts are considered to be in the hotel business for tax purposes, instead of the real estate rental business (see "Social Security and Medicare Taxes," above). If you fall within this group, you aren't subject to the NII tax. However, you are required to pay Social Security and Medicare taxes on your net rental income. At income levels above $200,000 for singles and $250,000 for marrieds filing jointly, you must pay a 3.8% Medicare tax, the same amount as the NII tax.

Local and State Occupancy Taxes

Your short-term rental activity is likely subject to occupancy taxes levied by your state, city, county, or other local government. These taxes go by different names—for example:

- occupancy tax
- transient occupancy/rental/lodging tax
- sales tax
- hotel tax

- lodging tax
- room tax
- gross receipts tax
- bed tax
- transaction privilege tax, or
- tourist tax.

These taxes are completely separate from income tax and are collected by your state and/or local government, not the IRS.

Most states now tax short-term rentals the same as stays at hotels. About 20 states have statewide hotel/occupancy taxes. Local occupancy taxes are also assessed by most cities and counties.

These taxes apply only to short-term home or room rentals—short-term is typically defined as rentals of 30 days or less. However, in some states short-term rentals are defined as less than 28 days, and in others— Florida, for example—as much as 185 days. Some areas have casual use rules that excuse rentals of only a few days per year from such taxes. Moreover, in some areas rentals of private homes are entirely exempt from these taxes.

The amount of local taxes varies, as does how they are calculated. They can be based on a flat fee, rental percentage, number of guests, number of nights guests stay, type of property involved, or a combination of any of these. On average, they equal about 12% of the income earned from the short-term rental (including rents, cleaning fees, and other fees). The taxes are typically due monthly or quarterly. The due dates can vary depending on the amount of tax owed.

> **EXAMPLE:** Brandon owns a home in Boise, Idaho, that he rents out on a short-term basis to state legislators while the Idaho Legislature is in session. Idaho requires guests who stay 30 nights or less to pay a 6% Idaho Sales Tax and a 2% Idaho Travel Convention Tax. Boise also imposes a 5% Greater Boise Auditorium District Tax. The total tax Brandon's guests must pay is 13% of the listing price (including cleaning fees).

You can find excellent summaries of the state and local short-term rental tax rules for each state on the Avalara website at https://mylodgetax.avalara.com/taxcenter/usa. You should also check your local government's website for information about these local taxes.

Local lodging taxes are ordinarily paid by the guests who pay for short-term rentals, not the hosts who provide them. This is the same as hotel occupancy taxes that are paid by a hotel's guests. The hosts' role is ordinarily limited to collecting the taxes from their guests and remitting them to the appropriate state and/or local agency. You may be required to register with your city or county, or obtain a business license, before collecting and remitting these taxes.

In many locations, Airbnb and VRBO have entered into agreements with the local governments involved to collect and remit occupancy taxes on behalf of hosts. In many areas this is done automatically; in other areas you must manually request this. You can find a list of the locations for which Airbnb automatically collects taxes at www.airbnb.com/help/article/2509/in-what-areas-is-occupancy-tax-collection-and-remittance-by-airbnb-available. The locations for which VRBO collects taxes are listed at https://help.vrbo.com/articles/What-Stay-Taxes-Lodging-Taxes-does-HomeAway-collect-and-remit.

Check your listings on the short-term rental platform(s) you use to determine for sure if sales taxes are being automatically collected. If not, you can usually manually direct the platform to collect the taxes. With Airbnb, for example, you can add taxes for a listing if you're using professional hosting tools, include the taxes within a special offer, or collect them from guests using the resolution center after check-in (see www.airbnb.com/help/article/2496/how-does-manual-occupancy-tax-collection-and-payment-work).

Note carefully, however, that Airbnb or VRBO may not collect all the occupancy taxes charged on your rental. They ordinarily collect state wide taxes and some local taxes. But they don't collect all city or county occupancy taxes for every location. You need to check with your city or county to determine if there are any local occupancy taxes due that your rental platform does not collect. You'll need to manually direct the platform to collect such taxes.

It is your responsibility to pay any occupancy taxes your rental platform does not collect. If you fail to do so, you'll be responsible for paying the tax and you could also be fined by your local tax authority.

If your rental platform does not collect and remit sales taxes for you, you can hire a private company to do so. Among these are Avalara (https://mylodgetax.avalara.com). You can also collect them yourself. You can include them in the nightly price you charge, or demand that they be paid directly to you in person in advance when your guests check in. It's a good practice to list the tax as a line item on the bill submitted to the guest. Alternatively, you can always choose to pay the taxes out of your own pocket instead of having your guests pay them. This can be an effective sales promotion (retailers sometimes pay their customers' sales taxes for this purpose). Whatever you do, you should make it clear to your guests prior to booking how much local tax they'll have to pay and how it must be paid. ●

Tax-Free Short-Term Rentals

ecades ago, Congress decided that people who rent their homes only a few days per year should not have to pay any tax on the income they earned. This rule was commonly known as the Masters exemption because it primarily benefited people who owned homes near major event sites, like the Masters Golf Tournament. However, with the advent of online rental platforms like Airbnb, more people than ever can take advantage of this little-known tax provision. Before you spend your tax-free windfall, there are a number of restrictive rules you need to understand.

Short-Term Rentals That Qualify for Tax-Free Treatment

The deceptively simple rule is that the income you earn is tax free if you rent out:

- a dwelling unit
- that you use as a residence
- for 14 days or less during the year. (I.R.C. § 280A(g).)

Dwelling Unit

A dwelling unit includes a house, apartment, condominium, mobile home, boat, or similar property, and all structures or other property accompanying it such as a garage or unattached studio. The property can be your main home, vacation home, or any other place you live. It makes no difference whether you own or rent the dwelling unit.

Each separate space that contains basic living accommodations (such as sleeping space, toilet, and cooking facilities) is considered a dwelling unit. Thus, a single building may contain more than one dwelling unit—for example, each of the two units in a duplex house is a separate dwelling unit. Likewise, if the basement of a house contains basic living accommodations, it is a separate dwelling unit. On other hand, a home's garage or backyard would not be a separate dwelling unit.

Used as a Residence

This tax exemption is intended to benefit people who rent out the homes where they live, not hotel or motel operators. Thus, to qualify for tax-free treatment, you must use the dwelling unit as your residence during the year. This requirement is not onerous. You automatically qualify if you personally use a dwelling for at least 34 days during the year. If you personally use the dwelling less than 34 days, it will still qualify as your residence if the home is used personally for (1) more than 14 days, or (2) more than 10% of the number of days during the year the property is rented for a fair rental, whichever is greater.

> EXAMPLE: Archie has a cabin in the woods that he lived in for 20 days during the summer and rented for ten days. The cabin qualifies as a residence because Archie lived in it more than 14 days.

Personal use of your home includes the time you and various family members stay at the property without paying rent. (See "Calculating Personal and Rental Days," in Chapter 9, for details on how to calculate your personal use days.) (I.R.C. § 280A(g).)

Rentals of 14 Days or Less

You qualify for tax-free treatment only if you rent a dwelling you use as a residence for 14 days or less during the year. If you rent the property for 15 days or more during the year, all your rental income is taxable—a big difference. Obviously, you need to keep careful track of your number of rental days and make sure not to exceed the magic number of 14.

A day is the 24-hour period for which a day's rental would be paid, not a calendar day. Thus, for example, a guest who stays in your home from Saturday afternoon through the following Saturday morning would be treated as having used the home for seven days even though the person was on the premises for eight calendar days. (IRS Reg. § 1.280A-1(f).) This is a great rule for hosts; otherwise, stays of one night could count as "two days" even if the host is paid for only one night.

Your property is "rented" if you charge your guests money to stay there. For purposes of the 14-day rental rule, property rented for less than fair market value is still considered as rented and counts toward determining the 14-day rental period.

> EXAMPLE: Kevin rents his condo to tourists through Airbnb for a total of ten days during the year, charging them market rates. He also rents the unit to his sister for seven days, charging her half what he could get through Airbnb. He must count the rental to his sister toward the 14-day limit, even though he didn't charge her market rate rent. He has a total of 17 days of rental use during the year, thus he does not qualify for tax-free treatment.

However, you don't need to count days you let guests stay at your property for free. For example, Kevin from the example above wouldn't have had to count his sister's stay if he didn't charge her rent.

Room Rentals

You don't need to rent out your entire home to qualify for tax-free treatment of your rental income; you can also rent a room or rooms in your home.

> EXAMPLE: Claudia owns and lives all year long in a two-bedroom Florida beachfront condominium—it is her only home. This year, she rents her second bedroom to tourists for 14 days during the summer through Airbnb. Her rental qualifies for tax-free treatment.

However, if the space you rent constitutes a separate dwelling unit, you must separately satisfy the personal use requirement—that is, you or a family member must live in it for 34 days or at least the greater of 14 days or 10% of the rental days.

> **EXAMPLE:** Gavin owns a home with a separate in-law unit in his basement. The unit has its own sleeping, bathroom, and kitchen facilities. The unit is a separate dwelling. Gavin lives in his main home full time; neither he nor any family members live in the in-law unit. Since he makes no personal use of the in-law unit, it cannot qualify for tax-free treatment.

Multiple Properties

You can own or rent more than one dwelling unit at a time during the year. Each dwelling can qualify as a residence if you live in it long enough—34 days, or at least 14 days or more than 10% of the rental days. Thus, it's quite possible to obtain tax-free treatment for the rental income you earn from multiple properties the same year. However, each property must separately qualify as a residence you rent no more than 14 days. You cannot combine or split rental days among multiple residences.

> **EXAMPLE:** Lisa owns a co-op apartment in New York City and a vacation home in Bangor, Maine. During the year, she lives in her New York City home for 300 days and in her Bangor home for 40 days. Both properties qualify as residences for Lisa. She rents her New York City home for seven days during the year and her Bangor home for 14 days. Both rentals qualify for tax-free treatment.

Multiple Hosts

A single dwelling may qualify for a maximum of 14 days of free rental income. Roommates who live in the same house or apartment together occupy a single dwelling, even if they have separate bedrooms—a bedroom by itself is not considered a dwelling. Thus, if you live with roommates in the same residence, each person is not entitled to his or her own 14 days of tax-exempt income.

> EXAMPLE: Abigail, Betty, and Cynthia live together in the same three bedroom home, each with her own bedroom. Each roommate rented out her bedroom for 14 days during the year. There were no days in which more than one bedroom was rented at a time. Together, the roommates rented their dwelling for 42 separate days. None of the roommates qualifies for tax-free treatment of their rental income because the dwelling was rented for more than 14 days during the year. Had each roommate rented her room for four days, instead of 14, the rentals would qualify for tax-free treatment because the dwelling would be rented for a total of only 12 days. Each roommate could pocket her rental income without paying income tax on it.

Since a bedroom is not a separate dwelling, renting two or more bedrooms at the same time does not change the number of days the dwelling is rented for purposes of the 14-day rule—for example, if you have a four-bedroom home, there is one day of rental use whether you rent one-bedroom or all four bedrooms on the same day.

> EXAMPLE: Abigail, Betty, and Cynthia all go on a 14 day vacation together. They rented out all three bedrooms in their apartment to three different people for the 14 days. Since the apartment was rented for no more than 14 days, the rental income the roommates earn qualifies for tax-free treatment.

Effect of Qualifying for Tax-Free Treatment

Here's what happens if you satisfy the conditions outlined above.

No Tax Due on Rental Income

If you meet the above requirements, all the rental income you receive is tax free, no matter how much you earn. As far as the IRS is concerned, it's as if the rental never occurred.

> **EXAMPLE:** Claudia owns a condo in Miami. This year she lived in it for 300 days and rented it out for 14 days, earning $1,400. She doesn't have to pay any federal tax on this income.

All but five states follow the federal rule in not imposing income tax on 14-day-or-less home rentals. The only states that tax such rentals are: Alabama, Arkansas, Mississippi, New Jersey, and Pennsylvania.

No Deductions for Tax-Free Rentals

Because they are tax-free, you get no extra tax deductions for 14-day-or-less short-term rentals. For example, you can't deduct the fees you pay to Airbnb or other rental platforms or deduct any other expenses you incur in renting out your property, such as cleaning, supplies, repairs, insurance, or depreciation. Instead, if you're a homeowner, you continue to take the normal personal tax deductions to which any homeowner is entitled—that is, you may deduct your real estate taxes and home mortgage interest as personal itemized deductions on IRS Schedule A. You may take these deductions whether you rent your main home or a second or vacation home. For 2018 through 2025, homeowners may deduct up to $10,000 in property tax each year on a main and second home. The mortgage interest deduction for homes purchased during this time period is limited to home acquisition debt up to $750,000. If you purchased your home before 2018, you may deduct the interest on up to $1 million in home acquisition debt. If you're a renter, you don't get these deductions.

> **EXAMPLE.** Assume that Claudia paid $5,000 in mortgage interest and $2,000 in taxes for her condo during the year. She also incurred $600 in expenses for her short-term rental—this included the fee she paid to Airbnb for her listing, items she provided to her guests, and repairs of her condo. She may deduct the taxes and interest as an itemized deduction on her Schedule A. She gets no deduction for the $600 in rental expenses, and no depreciation deduction.

Reporting Tax-Free Rental Income on Your Tax Return

In theory, because income from annual rentals of 14 days or less is tax free, you don't have to list it as income on your tax return. This means you don't need to file IRS Schedule E, the tax form landlords file to report their income and expenses, because your home is not considered a rental property for tax purposes. The instructions to Schedule E expressly provide for this. However, as a practical matter, if Airbnb or another rental platform you use reports your rental income to the IRS on a Form 1099-K or 1099-NEC (Form 1099-MISC was used before 2021), you could have problems with the IRS. IRS computers match the income shown on these forms with the income you report on your Form 1040. Thus, if you don't include the rental income on your return, the IRS may question you about it. This doesn't mean the income is taxable, it just means the IRS may ask you about it—likely through correspondence. You'd then have to explain to the IRS that the income was not taxable.

Under the procedures currently followed by Airbnb and other rental platforms (see Chapter 11), it's not likely your rental income will be reported to the IRS if you rent your property for 14 days or less during the year. However, if you do receive a Form 1099 reporting such income (with a copy automatically sent to the IRS), you should take steps to avoid questions from the IRS. The IRS has provided no guidance on how to deal with this problem, but one approach is to file Schedule E with your return and list the rental income on Line 3 as Rents received. Then, on Line 19 (Other) list the income as an expense and add the following note in the space provided on Line 19: "Rent on Line 3 is exempt from tax under Section 280A(g)—residence rented less than 15 days." You then list zero in Line 26 Total rental real estate and royalty income or (loss). This should satisfy IRS computers since the income shown on the 1099 will be listed on your return.

Keep records showing that your rental met the tax-free criteria, including a copy of your rental agreement, the dates the home was rented, and the amount of rent charged. ●

Deducting Your Expenses: The Basics

I f your short-term rental activity is not tax free, you're entitled to deduct your expenses from your rental income to determine how much of your income is subject to tax—also called net rental income. Virtually all the expenses you incur to rent your property are deductible. The rules about when and how to deduct your expenses vary according to the type of expense involved; unfortunately, these rules can get quite complicated.

What You Can Deduct

The tax law recognizes that when you rent your property, even if you do so only part time, you must spend money for things like mortgage interest, repairs, rental platform fees, maintenance, and many other expenses. The law allows you to subtract these expenses, plus an amount for the depreciation of your property, from your effective gross rental income (all the money actually earned from renting the property). You use that to determine your taxable income—which is the amount, if any, that you pay tax on.

For purposes of simplicity, we'll divide the expenses short-term rental hosts can deduct into the following categories:

- operating expenses
- repairs
- long-term asset expenses, and
- pass-through tax deduction.

This section provides an introduction to each of these categories (they are covered in greater detail in later chapters).

Operating Expenses

Operating expenses are the day-to-day expenses you incur for your short-term rental activity. They include things like mortgage interest if you own your home, rent if you're a renter, insurance, utilities, Airbnb or other similar fees and commissions, advertising costs, supplies, travel expenses, and car expenses. These types of expenses are currently deductible—that is, you can deduct them all in the same year when you pay them. They are covered in detail in Chapter 5.

Repairs and Maintenance

Repairs and maintenance are the costs you incur to keep your property up and running. Like operating expenses, they are always currently deductible in the year in which you incur them. Repair expenses are among the most valuable deductions you'll have. However, some of the changes you make to your property are not considered to be repairs for tax purposes; instead, they are improvements that may have to be deducted much more slowly than repairs. It's important to know the difference. There are also some special rules you can take advantage of that allow you to deduct expenses for improvements in a single year. Repair expenses are covered in detail in Chapter 6.

Long-Term Asset Expenses

Long-term assets are things you use for your rental activity that have a useful life of more than one year. Your main long-term asset is your home or building you rent out. However, long-term assets also include such things as furniture, appliances, vehicles, and equipment. These costs, called capital expenses by accountants, are considered to be part of your investment in your rental activity, not day-to-day operating expenses.

The general rule is that the cost of long-term assets must be deducted a little at a time over several years—a process called depreciation. Residential rental buildings (and structural components) are depreciated over 27.5 years. Commercial buildings are depreciated over 39 years. Long-term personal property assets are depreciated over a much shorter period—for example, furniture and appliances are depreciated over five years. Most taxpayers prefer to deduct their expenses as quickly as possible. Fortunately, you can avoid regular depreciation and deduct the full cost of most personal property you buy for your rental activity in a single year using 100% bonus depreciation or Section 179 of the tax code (see Chapter 7).

Pass-Through Tax Deduction

For 2018 through 2025, short-term hosts may qualify for a special pass-through tax deduction. This enables them to deduct from their income taxes up to 20% of their net income from their rental activity. (See Chapter 8.)

You Must Allocate Many Expenses Between Your Rental and Nonrental Use

Determining just how much you can deduct can get complicated when you rent out your home or property but live in it as well. This is because you can only deduct your expenses that relate to your rental use of the property. You are never allowed to deduct personal living expenses as rental expenses (although some home ownership expenses, such as mortgage interest are deductible as personal itemized deductions). As a result, you'll have to figure out what part of an expense that relates to the entire home can be deducted as a rental expense. For example, if you rent out your entire home for part of the year, you'll only be able to deduct your utility expenses for the days you rented out your home. If you rent a room or rooms in your home while you continue to live there, you'll have to further allocate your expenses according to the amount of space in your home that you rent out. Moreover, if there are any repairs or expenses that only relate to personal areas of the home, you won't be able to deduct those at all.

Any expenses that are just for your short-term rental activity—Airbnb fees, for example—can be deducted in full.

How to allocate and calculate your deductions is covered in Chapter 9.

How Your Tax Status Affects Your Deductions

Being a short-term rental host can be a business for tax purposes, an investment, or, in some cases, a not-for-profit activity, also called a hobby. Hosts whose rental activities qualify as a business are entitled to all the tax deductions discussed in this book. However, those whose rentals are an investment lose certain useful deductions. Tax deductions are extremely limited for hosts who, in the eyes of the IRS, are operating a not-for-profit activity. Your tax status is determined by how much time and effort you put into your rental activity, and whether you earn profits each year or act like you want to. Most short-term rental activities qualify as for-profit businesses.

Is Your Rental Activity a Business?

You want your rental activity to be viewed as a business by the IRS. Luckily, most rentals qualify as businesses. Indeed, it should be easier for most short-term rentals to qualify as businesses than regular long-term residential rentals.

Here's the basic rule you need to understand: Owning rental property qualifies as a business if you do it to earn a profit and work at it regularly and continuously. (*Commissioner v. Groetzinger*, 480 U.S. 23 (1987); *Alvary v. United States*, 302 F.2d 790 (2d Cir. 1962).)

Applying this rather vague test is a highly factual determination. The IRS says the relevant factors that can be considered include, but are not limited to:

- the type of rented property (commercial versus residential property)
- the number of properties rented
- the owner's or the owner's agent's day-to-day involvement
- the types and significance of any ancillary services provided under the lease
- the terms of the lease (for example, a short-term versus long-term lease), and
- whether the landlord has filed all required information returns (Form 1099-NEC; see Chapter 11). (Preamble to IRS Reg. 1.199A-1.)

There is no specific number of rental properties or rental units you must own for your rental activity to qualify as a business. Indeed, the tax court ruled back in 1946 that rental of one single-family residential unit constituted a business. The IRS agreed to follow this case (GCM 38779 (7/27/81) and the tax court continues to follow it throughout the country except the northeast. Moreover, the IRS has recently stated that "rental of a single property may require regular and continuous involvement such that the rental activity is a trade or business." (Preamble to IRS Reg. § 1.1411, TD 9644, https://federalregister.gov/a/2013-28410.) However, the IRS and courts have also said that renting of a single unit (or more) doesn't always constitute a business—it all depends on the facts and circumstances.

There is also no established minimum number of hours you must work for your rental activity to be a business. Nor do you have to do all the work yourself: You can hire a manager to help you and still qualify as a business as long as the manager or other person you hire works regularly and continuously.

In one case, for example, a married couple was found to be engaged in business even though all they owned was a 25% time-share interest in two condominium units and the actual work of renting out the units and keeping them in repair was performed by a management company. (*Murtaugh v. Comm'r.*, T.C. Memo 1997-319.)

Thus, if you rent out your home, vacation home, a room in your home, or any other property though Airbnb or a similar online rental platform, you're engaged in a business for tax purposes if your activity is undertaken to earn a profit and carried on regularly and continuously. For example, someone who has an extra bedroom in their house that they actively list on Airbnb or another online rental platform and rent at market rates to multiple guests during the year would likely be engaged in business, particularly if a profit is earned on the rentals. This is true whether they manage their short-term rentals themselves or hire a management company to do so for them.

Indeed, renting out residential property to multiple short-term guests during the year through online portals like Airbnb arguably requires much more continuous, systematic, and regular effort than renting to long-term residential tenants. Short-term rental hosts must constantly seek new guests and deal with their rapid turnover. They typically provide guests with amenities and services that traditional landlords do not, such as toiletries, linens, food, books, and many other items. More cleaning, maintenance, and repairs are typically required for short-term rentals.

Is Your Rental Activity an Investment?

Although there is no minimum number of days you have to rent a property to be in business, your rental activity must be continuous and regular to qualify as a business. Sporadic or irregular activities that make money are investments, not businesses. Thus, it's possible that a short-term host who rents a room or home for only a handful of days per year, or on a very occasional basis could be viewed as engaged in an investment activity, not a business. In that situation, however, if the total rentals added up to 14 days or less in one year, they likely wouldn't be subject to taxes anyway (see Chapter 3). And more than that would probably make the activity regular enough to qualify as a business.

The type of rental activities that are more likely to fall into the investment category are long-term rentals that require minimal management or work for the owner. For example, the IRS found that someone who inherited a house occupied by a long-term tenant was engaged in an investment activity when he continued to rent the property to the same tenant for another 14 years. The IRS and court found that although the owner (or his agent) took care of certain things like replacing the furnace, the management activities were too minimal to rise to the level of a business. Most short-term rental hosts put a lot more time and effort into managing their rentals because of the work required in continually having to get new guests and do the cleaning and extra work associated with a higher turnover of guests.

If your activity is an investment, not a business, you'll still be entitled to claim most of the deductions covered in this book. However, you won't be entitled to claim any of the following deductions:

- the pass-through tax deduction
- business start-up expenses
- Section 179 expensing
- the home office deduction, and
- rental investment seminars, conventions, or meetings.

Is Your Rental Activity Not for Profit?

In some cases, people who rent their property aren't really interested in earning a profit. They have other motives, such as providing cheap or free housing to relatives or having a place to take vacations. If the IRS determines that the primary motive you have for renting your property is something other than earning money, it will be classified as not-for-profit activity for tax purposes. Such activities are also referred to as hobbies.

As a result of the Tax Cuts and Jobs Act, having your short-term rental activity classified as a hobby is truly a tax disaster. As a result of the new law, during 2018 through 2025, you cannot deduct any of the expenses you incur from a hobby from your income taxes. But you're still required to report and pay tax on all the income you earn!

> EXAMPLE: Billy rents out his Las Vegas condo short-term to friends and family for free or at below-market rates. This IRS determines the activity is a hobby. In 2020, he earned $3,000 in short-term rental income and had $6,000 in expenses. He may not deduct the $6,000 expenses, but he must pay tax on the entire $3,000 income he earned.

Clearly, you want to avoid hobby status for your short-term rental activity at all costs. If you earn a profit from your rentals in three out of five consecutive years, the IRS must presume that you have a profit motive. Any legitimate profit—no matter how small—qualifies; you don't have to earn a particular amount or percentage. The presumption that you are engaged in a for-profit activity applies to your third profitable year and extends to all later years within the five-year period beginning with your first profitable year. However, you don't have to earn profits every year to be profit-motivated. Many people who want to earn profits from real estate rentals have negative cash flows. In one case, for example, an Oklahoma couple who owned a vacation condo in Hawaii that they rented out part time were found to be profit motivated even though they lost money for 11 of 13 years. The tax court was swayed by the fact that they earned a small profit for the prior two years; moreover, they spent a lot of time and money to remodel the condo, and after that their gross rental income rose significantly. (*McKinney v. Comm'r*, TC Memo 1981-181.)

But, if you keep incurring losses, the IRS could claim your short-term rental activity is not-for-profit. This is especially likely if you list your property on Airbnb or other rental platforms but never actually rent it to short-term guests, or rent it very rarely. In one recent case, for example, a couple's Florida vacation condominium was found to be a not-for-profit activity where they made no bona fide efforts to rent it other than listing it with a real estate broker who never actually showed it to anyone (*Redisch v. Comm'r*, T.C. Memo 2015-95). The moral: Simply listing your property on Airbnb or another rental platform will not make it a business (or even an investment) activity. To show the IRS that you're profit motivated, you should take the following steps:

- Keep good business records (see Chapter 13).
- Keep track of the time you spend on your rental activity.
- Keep a separate checking account for your rental activity.
- Take steps to increase your short-term rental income—for example, redo your online rental listing with better photos, offer more amenities to your guests, and make your property available for rent more often.
- Educate yourself about earning profits from short-term rentals by attending educational seminars and other programs.
- Prepare a business plan showing how much money you expect to earn or lose over the next several years.

Deductions for Multiple Owners

It's not uncommon for two or more friends, relatives, or others to purchase a vacation home or other property together that they rent out part time. If real property is owned by more than one person, the income and deductions from the rental of the property must be allocated among them according to their ownership interests.

Co-Owners Not Married to Each Other

Where co-owners take title to the property together as tenants in common or, more rarely, joint tenants, each co-owner owns an undivided interest in the entire property. In the case of a tenancy in common, the interests can be equal or divided in unequal amounts—whatever the owners agree upon. The ownership interest of each owner should be listed on the property deed.

> EXAMPLE: Al and Alice, brother and sister, buy a vacation home together, taking title as tenants in common. They decide that because Al put more money down on the property, he should own a 60% interest and Alice 40%. This means that Al is legally entitled to 60% of the rental income the property generates and is supposed to pay 60% of the expenses. Alice gets the remaining 40%.

Although they own rental property together, each cotenant reports their share of the income and deductions from the rental property on their own tax return, filing Schedule E. Each owner's share is based on his or her ownership interest—for example, Alice in the example above lists her 40% share of the income and deductions from the co-owned vacation home on her Schedule E and pays tax on that amount. Al lists the other 60% on his own Schedule E. If one cotenant pays more than his or her proportionate share of the expenses, the overpayment is treated as a loan to the other cotenants and may not be deducted. The cotenant who overpays is legally entitled to be reimbursed by the other cotenants. (T.C. Memo 1995-562.)

Co-Ownership by Spouses

Spouses typically take title to real property they own together as joint tenants—rather than tenants in common. Joint tenants are treated exactly the same as tenants in common for tax purposes, but there are significant nontax differences. Joint tenants must own the property 50-50. If a married couple that jointly owes rental property files a joint income tax return, as most do, they are treated as a single taxpayer by the IRS. The spouses' shares of the income and deductions from the rental property are combined on their single joint tax return. The couple reports their income and deductions from the jointly owned property on a single Schedule E they file with their joint return.

Ownership Through a Business Entity

Instead of taking title to property as individuals in their own names, multiple owners can form a business entity to own the property. This is ordinarily done to avoid personal liability for lawsuits—for example, if someone slips and falls at the property. Typically, a "pass-through" business entity is chosen to own real property. Such an entity pays no taxes itself, although it must file an annual information return with the IRS. Instead any income or loss from property the entity owns is passed through to its owners who include the amount on their own personal tax returns. They share in these profits or losses according to their ownership interest in the entity. There are three main types of pass-through entitles: S corporations, partnerships, and limited liability companies (LLCs). LLCs are by far the most popular type of entity for owning rental property. LLCs with more than one owner are ordinarily treated the same as partnerships for tax purposes. LLCs with one owner are "disregarded entities"—the owner reports profits, losses, and deductions from rental activities on his or her individual Schedule E.

> **EXAMPLE:** Coworkers Arlene, Bill, and Charlie purchase a vacation cabin at Lake Tahoe that they rent out several weeks per year. They form a Nevada LLC called ABC, Ltd. to own and operate the property. They each have a one-third ownership interest in the LLC. Thus, one-third of the net rental income or loss from the property is passed through to each of them. Each year, the LLC must file IRS Form 1065, *U.S. Return of Partnership Income*, and provide each owner with an IRS Schedule K-1, *Partner's Share of Income, Deductions, Credits, etc.*, listing the owners' shares of the LLC's income and expenses. The owners must then file IRS Schedule E with their individual income tax returns, showing their share of income or losses from the LLC's activities.

Operating Expenses

This chapter is about the day-to-day operating expenses you incur for your short-term rental activity. All these expenses are currently deductible in the year they're incurred (except for start-up expenses). Some are deductible in full, others must be allocated according to how much and how long you rent your property.

What Are Operating Expenses?

You may start to deduct your operating expenses the moment your short-term rental activity begins—this is ordinarily when you list your property for short-term rental. Expenses you incur before you offer your property for rent are not operating expenses, but may be deductible as start-up expenses (see "Start-Up Expenses," below). There are many different types of operating expenses—so many, they can't all be individually listed in the tax law. The basic rule is that you can deduct in a single year any expense that is:

- ordinary and necessary
- current
- directly related to your rental activity, and
- reasonable in amount. (I.R.C. § 162.)

An expense is ordinary and necessary if it is common, helpful, and appropriate for your activity. It doesn't have to be indispensable—it need only help your rental activity in some way, even a minor way. A one-time expenditure can be ordinary and necessary. Generally, the IRS won't second guess your claim that an expense is ordinary and necessary unless the item or service clearly has no legitimate business purpose. You will not be allowed to deduct off-the-wall or clearly ridiculous expenses.

An expense is current if it is for an item that will benefit your rental activity for less than one year. These are the costs of keeping your rental venture going on a day-to-day basis, including money you spend on items or services that get used up, wear out, or become obsolete in less than one year. A good example of a current expense is the cost of utilities like electricity, gas, and water you provide your short-term guests. Anything you purchase that will benefit your rental activity for more than one year is not a current expense—for example, purchasing a new refrigerator for your vacation home. You can usually deduct the cost of personal property like a refrigerator in a single year using bonus depreciation or the de minimis safe harbor (see Chapter 7).

An expenditure must be *directly related to your rental activity* to be deductible as an operating expense. This means that you cannot deduct personal expenses. If you buy something for both personal and rental use, you can deduct only the business portion of the expense. You must figure out how much of the time you used the item for rental purposes and how much for personal purposes. You then allocate the total cost between the two purposes, and deduct only the rental portion of the cost. These allocation rules are particularly important for part-time rentals and are discussed in detail in Chapter 9.

Finally, unreasonable expenses are not deductible. As a rule of thumb, an expense is reasonable unless there are more economical and practical ways to achieve the same result. If the IRS finds that your deductions are unreasonably large, it will disallow them or at least disallow the portion it finds unreasonable. Certain areas are hot buttons for the IRS—especially travel and meal expenses. The IRS won't allow any lavish expenses here, and you will have to follow strict rules requiring you to fully document these deductions.

Direct Expenses Deductible in Full

Any operating expense you incur solely for your short-term rental activity is deductible in full. These are expenses you incur only because you're renting your property short-term; otherwise, you wouldn't have them. This includes all the following types of expenses.

Rental Platform Fees and Commissions

The fees charged by short-term rental platforms, such as Airbnb, VRBO, or FlipKey, are all fully deductible operating expenses. These fees can be substantial, so this can be a valuable deduction. For example, Airbnb charges a "host service fee" equal to 3% of the cost of each reservation, while VRBO charges $499 for an annual subscription. These rental platforms also typically charge "service fees" to guests—for example, Airbnb charges guests a 6%–12% service fee. Obviously, these fees are not deductible by hosts since they don't pay them. Guests may be able to deduct such fees if their travel is for business.

Local and State Licenses and Fees

Many local (and some state governments) require short-term hosts to pay for business licenses and special registration fees. For example, San Francisco requires short-term hosts to pay a $250 registration fee every two years. These fees are fully deductible operating expenses.

Advertising and Marketing Expenses

Expenses you incur to advertise and market your short-term rental are fully deductible. For example, if you hire a professional photographer to take pictures of your property for your online rental listing, the cost is fully deductible. The same goes for hiring a copywriter to help you write the description of your property for your listing. If you create your own website to market your short-term rental, the cost is also deductible. Ongoing website hosting, maintenance, and updating costs are a currently deductible operating expense. Money you spend to get people to view your website, such as SEO (search engine optimization) campaigns, is also currently deductible. However, the cost of initially developing your website may constitute a capital expense, not a currently deductible business operating expense. If so, the cost may have to be deducted over three years. Any other advertising you do is also deductible.

Car and Local Transportation Expenses

Local travel is travel by car or other means within the area of your tax home—the entire city or general area where you live. If the home you rent out short-term is also the main home where you live, this deduction may be quite limited. You may have more deductions if you have a second home you rent out, but even here there are restrictions.

Driving Must Be for Rental Activity

You may only deduct local travel if it's for your short-term rental activity. For example, you can deduct the cost of driving to the airport to pick up or drop off your short-term guests. You can also deduct driving to meet with repair people, attorneys, accountants, property managers, and other people who help in your short-term rental activity.

What about travel to and from your short-term rental property? If this property is also your main home (that is, the place where you live), you'll likely have no deductions for this unless you have an office outside your home you use to manage your rental activity (which is rare for short-term rental hosts). In this event, you could deduct travel to and from your outside office to your main home for rental purposes.

You'll likely qualify for more deductible local travel expenses if you rent out a property other than your main home, such as a vacation home. Travel from your main home to your vacation home (or other property away from your own home) can be deductible if done for rental purposes—for example, to do cleanup, maintenance, repairs, guest check-in, hauling supplies, or other rental-related tasks. However, this is true only if you have an office in your main home that qualifies as the principal place of business for your rental activity (see "Home Office Deduction," below). Otherwise, such trips are nondeductible personal commuting, even if there is a rental purpose for the trip. Moreover, you may not currently deduct driving expenses incurred while making improvements to your home or other property you use in your short-term rental activity. Instead, the cost of such driving must be added to the basis (cost) of the improvement and depreciated over several years (see Chapter 6).

How to Deduct Car Expenses

If you have tax deductible driving expenses, you may deduct them by using the standard mileage rate or the actual expense method. With the standard mileage rate, you deduct a specified number of cents for every business mile you drive. The IRS sets the standard mileage rate each year. For 2020, the rate is 57.5¢ per mile. To figure out your deduction, simply multiply your rental miles by the applicable standard mileage rate. You can find the current standard mileage rate on the IRS website. Alternatively, instead of using the standard mileage rate, you can deduct the actual cost of using your car for your rental activity. This requires more record keeping, but it can result in a larger deduction. If you use this method, you must keep careful track of all the costs you incur for your car during the year, including:

- gas and oil
- repairs and maintenance
- depreciation of your original vehicle and improvements
- license and registration fees
- parking fees for rental-related trips, and
- insurance and auto club dues.

You may deduct parking fees and tolls with either method.

You must use the standard mileage rate in the first year you use a car for your rental activity, or you are forever foreclosed from using that method for that car. If you use the standard mileage rate the first year, you can switch to the actual expense method in a later year. Whichever method you use, you must keep track of all the driving you do for your rental activity (see Chapter 13).

Long Distance Travel Expenses

Long distance travel is travel away from the area of your tax home (the city or general area where you live) that requires you to stay at least overnight at your destination before returning home. If the property you rent to short-term guests is a vacation home or another home outside the area of your tax home, you may have substantial long distance travel expenses. Such expenses can be deductible. However, you can't deduct trips primarily for personal vacations.

What Travel Is Deductible?

To be deductible, your trip must be primarily for your rental activity. This means that you must have a rental purpose in mind before starting out, and you must actually spend over half your time working at your short-term rental activity while you're away. Examples of rental purposes include:

- traveling to your property to deal with guests, maintenance, or repairs
- traveling to building supply stores or other places to obtain materials and supplies for your rental activity
- learning new skills to help in your rental activity, by attending landlord-related classes, seminars, conventions, or trade shows, and
- traveling to see people who can help you operate your rental activity, such as attorneys, accountants, or real estate managers.

For example, an Oklahoma couple owned a vacation condo in Hawaii that they rented to short-term guests for many years. The IRS and Tax Court ruled that their travel and meal expenses for their two and three-week trips to Hawaii over a two-year period were not deductible because the trips were primarily vacations. Although they spent some time repairing and refurbishing their condo, they failed to show that this was the primary reason for their travel and meal expenses. (*McKinney v. Comm'r*, T.C. Memo 1981-181.)

You may not currently deduct travel expenses incurred in order to make improvements to property you use in your short-term rental activity—for example, travel expenses related to adding a new roof to your vacation home. Instead, the cost of such travel must be added to the basis (cost) of the improvement and depreciated over several years (see Chapter 6).

What Expenses Can You Deduct?

If your travel is deductible, you may deduct transportation expenses—that is, the expenses you incur travelling to your destination, such as plane fare. You may also deduct the expenses you incur to stay alive (food and lodging) and do rental business while at your destination. Such destination expenses include:

- hotel or other lodging expenses for rental business days (if any)
- 50% of meal and beverage expenses

- laundry and dry cleaning expenses, and
- tips you pay on any of the other costs.

You may deduct 100% of your transportation expenses if you spend *more than half of your time* on rental activities while at your destination. In other words, your rental activity days must outnumber your personal days. If you spend more time on personal activities than on rental activities, you get no transportation deduction. You may also deduct the destination expenses you incur on days when you spend most of your time on rental-related tasks. Expenses incurred on personal days at your destination are nondeductible personal expenses.

You may deduct the travel costs of your spouse or any other relative who is a co-owner of the rental property you travel to visit as long as that person spends sufficient time on rental activities. If you bring your family along simply to enjoy the trip, you may still deduct your own business expenses as if you were traveling alone.

Calculating Time Spent on Rental Activities While Away From Home

To calculate how much time you spend on rental activities while on a trip, compare the number of days you spend on rental-related work to the number of days you spend on personal activities. You spend a day on rental activities if you:

- spend more than four hours doing rental-related work—for example, working on repairs or maintenance of the property or dealing with your short-term guests
- spend more than four hours on travel for your rental activity (travel time begins when you leave home and ends when you reach your destination, or vice versa)
- drive at least 300 miles for your rental activity. You can average your mileage. For example, if you drive 600 miles to your destination in two days, you may claim two 300-mile days, even if you drove 500 miles on one day and 100 miles on the other
- spend more than four hours on some combination of travel and your rental activities, and

- stay at your destination between days you work on rental activities, if it would have cost more to go home and return than to remain where you are. This sandwich rule allows you to count weekends as rental activity days, if you work at your travel destination during the previous and following week.

EXAMPLE: Bill lives in Boston and owns a two-bedroom vacation home in Miami that he rents short-term through Airbnb and other rental platforms. This year, he flew from home to Miami and spent five days working on repairing and remodeling the home and then flew back home. He spent five hours each day on this work. His trip was primarily for his rental business activity. He may deduct his airfare and 50% of his meals while in Miami.

Home Office Deduction

If your rental activity qualifies as a business for tax purposes (see Chapter 4), you may able to take the home office deduction. This enables you to deduct as a rental expense a portion of your rent or home mortgage, utilities, and other home expenses. In addition, you'll be able to deduct driving from home to your rental property (if other than your main home). To qualify for this deduction, you must pass three tests:

1. **Exclusive Use Test:** You must use a portion of your home exclusively for your rental business. If you use part of your home—such as a room or studio—as your rental business office, but you also use that space for personal purposes, you won't qualify for the home office deduction. You can use an entire room or rooms for your office, or just part of a room. Since your use must be exclusive, your guests must not be allowed to use the space while they stay in your home. This should pose no problem where your office is in your main home and you rent out a vacation home or other property you have. However, the IRS might have trouble believing you satisfy the exclusive use requirement where your office is in your main home and you rent the entire home to short-term guests and are not present (unless you can show you have a good lock on the door to your home office that you keep locked).

2. **Regular Use Test:** You must also use your home office regularly for your rental business. The IRS doesn't say exactly how much this is, but you should use your home office at least a few hours every week.

3. **Business Importance Test:** Finally, your home office has to serve an important function in your rental business. You'll qualify if you:

   - regularly and exclusively use your home office for administrative or management activities for your rental business, and
   - use no other fixed location to regularly conduct these activities. Administrative or management activities include, but are not limited to: keeping books and records, ordering supplies, scheduling appointments, talking to guests or a property manager on the phone, arranging for repairs, or writing. Provided you have no other fixed location where you regularly do these things—for example, an outside office—you'll get the deduction.

If you pass all three tests, you then need to determine what percentage of your home you use for business. Divide the square footage of your home office by the total square footage of your home. For example, if your home is 1,600 square feet and you use 400 square feet for your home office, 25% of the total area is used for business. You can deduct your home office percentage of your rent, mortgage and property taxes, depreciation, utilities, home maintenance, insurance, and other home expenses. However, you cannot deduct more than the annual net profit you earn from your rental business. If your deductions exceed your profits, you can deduct the excess in the following year and in each succeeding year until you deduct the entire amount.

Alternatively, you may use a simplified method to calculate your deduction. With this method you deduct $5 for each square foot of your office. However, if you use this method your deduction is limited to $1,500 per year, no matter how big your office.

Hiring Help

The cost of any help you hire solely to aid with your short-term rental activity is fully deductible. For example, you can deduct the cost of hiring a property management company to manage your short-term rental activity. The cost of workers who provide services for your entire home must be allocated between your rental and nonrental use of the property. For example, you would have to allocate the cost of hiring a gardener, pool maintenance person, or housekeeper who cleans your entire home.

Legal and Professional Services

Legal and professional services for rental activity are fully deductible. For example, you can deduct the cost of hiring an attorney to draft a short-term rental agreement for you. You can also deduct the cost of hiring a firm to process and pay any local lodging taxes due on your rentals. You may deduct any accounting fees that you pay for your rental activity as a deductible operating expense—for example, fees you pay an accountant to set up or keep your books, prepare your tax return, or give you tax advice for your rental activity.

You may also deduct the cost of having an accountant or other tax professional complete the rental portion of your tax return—Schedule E and other rental activity tax forms—but you cannot deduct the time the preparer spends on the personal part of your return. Make sure that you get an itemized bill showing the portion of the tax preparation fee allocated to preparing your Schedule E.

Guest Amenities

It's common for short-term rental hosts to provide their guests with various amenities such as linens, sheets, soaps, shampoo, toothpaste, toothbrushes, razors, toilet paper, paper towels, games, guidebooks, first aid kits, and other supplies, and even food. All such items are fully deductible if they are purchased only for your guests' use. If you also use them, the cost must be allocated. You may also deduct the cost of a second (or more) phone line you provide for your guests' use. You may not deduct the cost of your first phone line, but you can deduct the costs of rental activity phone calls you make from this line—this requires you to keep track of how much you use the phone for rental and nonrental calls.

Gifts

Gifts you provide to your short-term guests or others in the course of your rental activity are deductible. However, the gift expense deduction is limited to $25 per person per year. Any amount over the $25 limit is not deductible.

No Charitable Deduction for Free Use of Short-Term Rentals

During the coronavirus (COVID-19) pandemic, some hosts made their short-term rentals available for free or at reduced rates to health care workers and others performing essential work. Unfortunately, if you're one of these hosts, you may not claim a charitable tax deduction for your good deeds.

You never qualify for a charitable tax deduction when you give something of value to an individual, even if the person is needy. You can only get a deduction when you give money or property to a tax-qualified 501(c)(3) charity. However, even if you make a short-term rental available for free to a charity, you likely still won't get a charitable deduction. IRS rules generally don't allow a charitable deduction for a contribution of less than your entire interest in property. The IRS says that a contribution of the right to use property is a contribution of less than your entire interest in that property and is not deductible. For example, the IRS does not allow a deduction when owners of vacation homes make them available as prizes in charity auctions.

Airbnb hosts have the option of donating a specified percentage of their payouts to the Open Homes Fund, which distributes grants to nonprofit partners of Airbnb's Open Homes Program. These are cash donations to a 501(c)(3) charity, not donations of the use or property; they are tax deductible. However, hosts must report their entire payout as income, and then deduct the portion they donate. A charitable deduction of $300 may be claimed by taxpayers who don't itemize their deductions. A charitable deduction over $300 is only available to taxpayers who itemize. Only about 10% of all taxpayers have enough personal deductions to itemize.

Entertainment Not Deductible

Before 2018, if you provided your guests with tickets to the theatre, sporting events, amusement parks, or similar events, you could deduct 50% of the cost. However, the Tax Cuts and Jobs Act eliminated almost all deductions for business-related entertainment starting in 2018. This doesn't mean you shouldn't provide your guests with free tickets or other forms of entertainment—it just means you can't deduct the cost.

Other Operating Expenses

Any other operating expenses you incur just for your rental activity are also fully deductible provided they are ordinary, necessary, and reasonable in amount—for example:

- any fees or service charges for PayPal or another online payment service that you use for your rental activity
- cleaning fees you pay to have the apartment professionally cleaned before and after your guests leave
- the cost of purchasing a lockbox or having duplicate keys made
- the cost of storing your belongings while guests stay in your apartment
- the cost of any credit reports you obtain to screen potential guests
- dues and subscriptions for your rental activity, and
- education directly related to your rental activity, such as a conference or seminar about how to make a profit from short-term rentals.

Start-Up Expenses

Start-up expenses are operating expenses you incur before you make your property available for rent. They are the costs you incur to get your rental business up and running. Start-up expenses include:

- minor or incidental repairs to get a rental property ready to rent
- home office expenses
- insurance premiums

- costs to create and set up a website
- business licenses, permits, and other fees, and
- fees paid to lawyers, accountants, consultants, and others for professional services.

Start-up expenses are not deductible in the same way as regular operating expenses. First, they are only deductible if your rental activity qualifies as a business for tax purposes. If so, you may deduct $5,000 in start-up expenses in the year you make your property available for rent. Any amount over $5,000 may be deducted in equal amounts over 180 months. However, you won't be entitled to the full $5,000 first-year deduction in the unlikely event you have more than $50,000 in start-up expenses. Your $5,000 deduction is reduced by the amount by which your start-up expenditures exceed the $50,000 limit. Obviously, you want to spend no more than the first-year limit on start-up expenses so you don't have to wait 15 years to get all of your money back.

Operating Expenses That Must Be Allocated

The following operating expenses are not deductible in full. Instead, they must be allocated (prorated) according to how much of your property you rent short-term and how much of the time you do so. How to perform these allocations is covered in detail in Chapter 9.

Rent

If you're a renter, you may deduct a portion of the rent you pay while short-term guests stay at your home. Residential rent is ordinarily not deductible, so this can be one of the biggest tax benefits of short-term rentals.

> EXAMPLE: Linda rents a two-bedroom apartment in San Francisco for $3,000 per month. She rents the entire apartment to short-term guests for 30 days during the year. She may deduct 30 days' rent, or $3,000, as a short-term rental expense.

However, make sure your landlord knows about and approves of your short-term rental activity because most residential leases restrict the ability of tenants to sublease the property without the landlord's approval. Thus, a tenant who engages in the short-term rental of the property without obtaining the landlord's permission could get evicted.

Home Mortgage Interest

If you have a mortgage on the home, vacation home, or other property you rent out short-term, you may deduct a portion of the interest as a rental expense (but not repayment of the principal amount of the loan). Any amount you can't deduct as a rental expense should be deducted as a personal itemized deduction.

> **EXAMPLE:** Bill rents his vacation home 50% of the time to short-term guests and uses it personally 50% of the time. He may deduct $6,000 of his $12,000 annual mortgage interest on the home as landlord expenses on his IRS Schedule E. He deducts the remaining $6,000 in interest as an itemized personal deduction on Schedule A.

However, home mortgage interest is not deductible as a personal itemized deduction if the home is used personally by the owner for less than 10% of the total days it's rented (or less than 14 days, if this is greater). (I.R.C. § 163(h)(4)(A)(i)(II).) For example, if a vacation home is lived in by the owner for 20 days and rented for 300, no personal itemized deduction for home mortgage interest may be claimed. For homes purchased in 2018 through 2025, the deduction for home mortgage interest is limited to acquisition loans for a main and second home totaling a maximum of $750,000. The amount is $1 million for first and second homes purchased before 2018.

Interest payments. Interest deducted as part of your short-term rental activity is not counted toward these limits, which can allow you to deduct more total interest.

EXAMPLE: Sally has a $1 million mortgage on a home she bought in January 2019 on which she pays $60,000 interest annually. She rented the home three months of the year to short-term guests, and lived in it nine months. Only interest on loan amounts up to $750,000 is deductible as an itemized deduction on Schedule A, so she can only deduct $33,750 of her $45,000 mortgage payments for the nine months she lived in the home. However, she can also deduct 100% of her mortgage interest for the three months she rented the home, or $15,000, as a rental expense not subject to the $750,000 limit. She gets a $15,000 deduction on Schedule E.

Credit Card and Loan Interest

If you use your credit card or take out a loan to purchase goods or services for your rental activity, you can deduct the interest you pay to the credit card company or lender, even if you have to depreciate the principal amount of the purchase. Such business interest is deductible in the year in which it is paid. If the item you purchase is used only part of the time for your rental activity, it will be only partly deductible.

EXAMPLE: Andre uses his credit card to purchase and install a $900 dishwasher in his home that he rents to short-term guests during 25% of the year. 25% of the credit card interest he pays on the $900 is deductible as it is paid.

Property Taxes

You can partly deduct your current year state and local property taxes on your home as an operating expense. For 2018 through 2025, the personal itemized deduction for property taxes is capped at $10,000 per year. Amounts deducted as a short-term rental expense don't count toward the annual limit. Thus, if you itemize your deductions, engaging in a short-term rental activity could help you deduct more property tax on your main or second home.

> EXAMPLE: Ed pays $12,000 per year in property tax on his home. He rents the home out 25% of the year to short-term guests through Airbnb. This enables him to deduct $3,000 of his property tax (25%) as part of his rental expense deduction on IRS Schedule E. He is able to itemize because all his personal deductions exceed the applicable standard deduction for the year ($12,200). He deducts the remaining $9,000 in property tax as a personal itemized deduction on his Schedule A. Had he not had a short-term rental activity, he could have deducted only $10,000 of his $12,000 in total property tax as a personal itemized deduction.

If you prepay the next year's property taxes, you may not deduct the prepaid amount until the following year. Real estate taxes imposed to fund specific local benefits for property, such as streets, sidewalks, sewer lines, and water mains, are not currently deductible as operating expenses where they are imposed only on the property owners who will benefit from them. Because these benefits increase the value of your property, you must add what you pay for them to the tax basis of your property and depreciate them.

Utilities

All your utility costs are partly deductible operating expenses that must be allocated according to your rental use. This includes electricity, water, gas, garbage pick-up, cable TV, Internet service, and snow removal costs. It also includes homeowners' association or condominium dues.

Parking

If you pay separately for parking where you live and allow your guests to use any of your parking spaces, you may deduct the portion of this expense allocable to your short-term rentals.

Insurance

You can deduct the rental portion of homeowners' insurance and renters' insurance premiums. You can also deduct the rental portion of private mortgage insurance (PMI) premiums for the property. If you prepay PMI premiums more than one year in advance, you can deduct only the premiums for the current year.

However, any insurance coverage you purchase just for your rental activity is fully deductible. For example, if you add an endorsement to your homeowners' policy to cover your short-term rentals, you can deduct 100% of the cost. Likewise, you can fully deduct the cost of a separate insurance policy for short-term rentals or full-blown landlord insurance coverage.

Casualty and Theft Losses

What happens if a short-term guest trashes your home or steals your property? It's possible that most or all of your loss will be covered by insurance or something like insurance. Many hosting companies have their own insurance or reimbursement plans. For example, Airbnb has a "host guarantee" in which it promises to pay up to $1 million to a host for property damage. However, Airbnb makes clear on its website that the guarantee is "not insurance," and does not cover cash and securities, collectibles, rare artwork, jewelry, pets, or personal liability. These losses will likely not be covered by your homeowners' insurance, which ordinarily excludes coverage for short-term rentals. To the extent any of them are not covered by insurance, you'll have a casualty or theft loss that could be deductible.

A casualty or theft loss is damage, destruction, or loss of property due to a sudden, unexpected, or unusual event caused by an external force. This includes, but is not limited to:

- vandalism, including vandalism to rental property by tenants
- theft
- earthquakes, fires, floods, landslides, sonic booms
- storms, including hurricanes and tornadoes
- government-ordered demolition or relocation of a building that is unsafe to use because of a disaster, and
- terrorist attacks.

You should file a police report when a theft occurs or if your property is vandalized.

Whether, and to what extent, such casualty losses are deductible is complicated. This is especially true if the property involved is used both by you personally and by your guests during your short-term rental activity, which will usually be the case. In this event, there are two separate casualty losses: one based on the personal use of the property and one based on the rental use.

The rules for deducting casualty losses to business and personal-use property differ greatly. Personal casualty losses are deducted as a personal itemized deduction on IRS Schedule A, while casualty losses to rental-use property are deducted on Schedule E. Additionally, personal casualty losses are deductible only if, and to the extent, they exceed 10% of the property owner's adjusted gross income and the first $100 is not deductible. Most importantly, however, during 2018 through 2025, the personal deduction for casualty losses is available only if the loss was caused by a federally declared disaster, such as a flood or hurricane. Other casualty losses to personal use property—for example, uninsured losses due to ordinary house fires—are not deductible. This rule does not apply to rental or other business use property—uninsured losses to such property are deductible as a rental or business expense whether or not caused by a federally declared disaster.

The IRS will need to provide guidance on how casualty losses are deducted where a residence is rented part of the year and also used personally part of the year by the owner and casualty loss is caused by an event other than a federally declared disaster.

Presumably, the pre-2018 rules will remain in effect for casualty losses due to federally declared disasters. Under these rules, short-term rental hosts subject to the vacation home rules—which includes most hosts— figure a casualty or theft loss as if they had not rented the property. The vacation home rules apply whenever you personally use the home you rent more than 14 days or 10% of the rental days (see Chapter 12).

Unless you rent your property for only 14 days or less for the year (or less than 10% of the rental days), you must complete Form 4684, *Casualties and Thefts*, treating all your casualty losses as personal losses. Your deductible rental loss is the amount, if any, that exceeds 10% of your adjusted gross income for the year (not including rental income). You may deduct the rental use percentage of this amount as a rental deduction on Schedule E. You may deduct any remaining portion of this amount as a personal casualty loss on Schedule A to the extent it exceeds 10% of AGI less $100.

> **EXAMPLE:** Host Shirley suffered a $10,000 rental loss to her residence when short-term guests damaged the property. She had a $50,000 AGI and rented her home 25% of the year. Her casualty loss rental deduction would be $10,000 loss – ($50,000 AGI x 10%) x 25% rental use = $1,250. She may deduct $3,650 of her remaining $8,750 casualty loss as a personal itemized deduction.

To calculate the total dollar value of the damage or loss to your property, you must always reduce your casualty losses by the amount of any insurance proceeds you receive, or reasonably expect to receive in the future. (I.R.C. § 165(h)(4)(E).) How much of an uninsured loss you can deduct depends on whether the property involved was stolen, completely destroyed, or partially destroyed. If more than one item is stolen, damaged, or destroyed, you must figure your deduction separately for each. If property is a total loss or stolen, you subtract its salvage value (if any) plus any insurance proceeds from its adjusted basis (original cost minus depreciation deductions plus improvements) to determine your deductible casualty loss; if your property is partially destroyed, your deductible loss is the decline in its fair market value, also reduced by any insurance proceeds. This decline can be based on the cost to repair the property or an appraisal.

> **EXAMPLE:** Shirley rented her Beverly Hills condo to a couple for the weekend through an online rental platform. When she returned, she discovered they threw a wild party during which her condo was completely trashed. Among other things, furniture was broken, toilets stopped up, carpets stained, and holes punched in the walls. An antique clock was also stolen. Shirley suffered a $25,000 casualty loss. The hosting company agreed to reimburse her for $15,000, leaving her with a $10,000 uninsured loss that she may deduct as a casualty loss.

For more details on deducting casualty losses, see IRS Publication 547, *Casualties, Disasters, and Thefts.* ●

Repairs

R epair expenses can be among your most valuable deductions. However, some of the changes you make to your property are not repairs at all; instead, they are improvements that must be deducted much more slowly than repairs. Additionally, the IRS says some repairs made for short-term room rentals are not deductible at all. And you'll need to know how to prorate certain repair expenses if you rent your property for only part of the year, or if you only rent a room or certain space in your house rather than the entire property. This chapter shows you how to recognize and maximize all your repair deductions.

Repairs vs. Improvements

The cost of repairs and routine maintenance to rental property are operating expenses that can be currently deducted in a single year. However, not all upkeep constitutes a repair for tax purposes. Some changes you make to your short-term rental property are capital improvements. Unlike repairs, improvements to real property (rental buildings and building components) cannot be deducted in a single year. Instead, their cost must be depreciated over 27 or 39 years.

In contrast, land improvements can usually be deducted in one year using bonus depreciation during 2018 through 2025. Improvements to personal property used in your short-term rental activity—for example, new appliances or carpeting in your home—can also usually be deducted in one year using bonus depreciation, Section 179 expensing, or the de minimis safe harbor. However, repairs still remain superior to improvements for tax purposes. (See "Why Repairs Are Better than Depreciation Deductions," below.)

It's up to you to decide whether an expense should be classified as a repair or an improvement. However, your decision is subject to review by the IRS. Unfortunately, telling the difference between a repair and an improvement isn't always easy. Indeed, for decades this issue has resulted in bitter disputes between business owners and the IRS. To help deal with this problem the IRS issued a lengthy set of regulations that took effect in 2014. These regulations lay out complicated rules for determining what constitutes a currently deductible repair versus a capital improvement that must be depreciated over several years. These "repair regulations" are covered below. Fortunately, however, they also include three safe harbors that may allow you to currently deduct all or most of your fix-up expenses, whether they are classified as repairs or improvements.

Why Repairs Are Better Than Depreciation Deductions

It's always better to deduct an expense as a repair (or using one of the safe harbors discussed below) than to depreciate the cost as an improvement. This is true even if 100% of the cost can be deducted in one year using bonus depreciation or Section 179 expensing (which can be done with personal property and land improvements but not building improvements; see Chapter 7). The reason repairs are better is that they are treated as a business operating expense. You get to deduct the full amount in the year the repair expense is incurred and there will be no tax impact when you later sell the property.

In contrast, when you deduct an expense through regular depreciation, bonus depreciation, or Section 179 expensing, the expense can result in extra tax when you sell the property. If you sell real property at a profit, you must pay tax at a rate up to 25% on your total depreciation deductions. If separately deducted personal property is involved, you pay tax on your regular or bonus depreciation or Section 179 deductions at your ordinary income tax rates (as much as 37%). This is called recapture, since deductions you previously took are recaptured into your income and taxed.

Your Personal Labor Is Not Deductible
You may never deduct the value of your own time and personal labor working on rental activities, whether the work is for a repair or an improvement. For example, if you spend 50 hours repainting your vacation home, you get no deduction for the value of your time. You may only deduct the cost of the paint, brushes, and other materials you use. This rule prevents the kind of abuse the IRS fears would happen if personal labor were deductible. You may deduct labor costs only when you hire other people to do the work and pay them for it. However, this doesn't mean you should never do any work on your property yourself. Although your personal labor is not deductible, you'll still save money by doing the work yourself because only a part of the money you deduct for labor costs ends up as a tax savings.

Deducting Repairs for Short-Term Room Rentals

If you rent your entire home on a short-term basis, you can deduct your repair expenses the same as any other landlord. Repairs to any portion of the property are deductible. You can also take advantage of the safe harbor rules covered below. You just have to allocate your expenses according to the amount of time you rent your property during the year. For example, if you rent your entire home 10% of the year, you may deduct 10% of the cost of deductible repairs. Such allocations are covered in detail in Chapter 9.

However, things are different if you rent only one or more bedrooms in your home, instead of the entire home. The IRS says that you can deduct repairs that benefit the entire property, subject to the allocation rules covered in Chapter 9. For example, you can deduct a portion of the cost of painting the entire home or repairing the water heater or the roof. You can also deduct repairs just for the bedroom or bedrooms (or other rooms) you rent—for example, fixing a window in a rental bedroom. However, the IRS has indicated in a proposed regulation that you may not deduct repairs for common areas when you only rent a room or rooms (IRS Proposed Regulation 1.280A-3(c)(2)). For example, if you rent a bedroom in your home while you continue to live in the home, you would not be able to deduct a repair to the kitchen sink, even if your guests were allowed to use the kitchen, because you also use the kitchen for personal purposes. This would be the most conservative and safest approach to take with common area deductions. Alternatively, you could decide to be more aggressive and deduct repairs to common areas when you rent a room in your home. After all, the proposed regulation cited above has not yet been adopted by the IRS (although it was promulgated in 1983!) and is not binding on taxpayers. However, you should consult with a tax professional before you do this.

Maintenance vs. Repairs

Maintenance is not the same thing as repairs. Maintenance is undertaken to prevent something from breaking down. A repair is done after a breakdown has occurred. For example, the cost of oiling the circulator pump in a hot water heater is maintenance; the cost of fixing an unlubricated pump that has failed is a repair. There is no practical tax difference between maintenance and repairs—they are both currently deductible operating expenses. However, because IRS Schedule E requires that you separately list what you spent for each category, you must keep track of these expenditures separately.

Three Safe Harbors

The IRS repair regulations contain three safe harbors that enable landlords (including short-term hosts) to currently deduct as a business operating expense certain building-related expenses:

- a safe harbor for small taxpayers
- the routine maintenance safe harbor, and
- the de minimis safe harbor.

If an expense comes within any safe harbor, and it is an ordinary and necessary expense, you may automatically treat the item as a currently deductible operating expense. You don't have to worry about whether the asset involved constitutes real property or personal property or whether the expense is for an improvement or repair—it's fully deductible (up to your rental use percentage) either way. And, since you're not taking a depreciation deduction, the deduction is not later subject to recapture when you sell your property.

You simply have to allocate the expense according to the rules covered in Chapter 9.

You always have the option of using the regular repair regulations if you wish. But the safe harbors are designed to make your life easier and simpler, and often enable you to deduct expenses that otherwise would have to be depreciated under the more complicated regular rules. Thus, you usually will want to take advantage of these safe harbors if you can. It's possible for an expense to fall within more than one safe harbor although you only need to come within one of them.

To determine whether an expense qualifies for a current deduction under the IRS's repair regulations, you can use a three-step approach:

1. Determine whether the expense qualifies as a current deduction under one of three new safe harbor tests.

2. If none of the safe harbors apply, determine whether the expense is a deductible repair or improvement under the regular repair versus improvement rules laid out in the IRS repair regulations.

3. If you determine the expense is for an improvement, determine if the asset is real property (building or building component) or personal property. If personal property, determine if you can deduct the expense in one year using the de minimis safe harbor, bonus depreciation, or Section 179 expensing. (See Chapter 7.)

When you are figuring out if an expense falls within a safe harbor, you should analyze it under the safe harbors in the order presented below.

Safe Harbor for Small Taxpayers (SHST)

The safe harbor for small taxpayers (SHST) is the single most important one. (IRS Reg. § 1.263(a)-3h.) If you qualify to use it, you may currently deduct as an operating expense on Schedule E all of your annual expenses for repairs, maintenance, improvements, and other costs for your rental subject to the allocation rules covered in Chapter 9. If so, you won't need to worry about any of the other safe harbors or the regular repair versus improvement regulations. To take advantage of this safe harbor, you need to keep careful track of all your annual expenses for repairs, maintenance, improvements, and similar items—something you should be doing anyway.

$1 Million Building Value Limit

The SHST may be used only for buildings—including condos and co-ops —with an unadjusted basis of $1 million or less. Unadjusted basis usually means a building's original cost (also called its cost basis), not including the cost of the land. (See Chapter 7 for a detailed discussion of how to determine a building's basis.) To determine a building's unadjusted basis, you don't subtract the annual amounts you deduct for depreciation. But you add the value of any improvements you make to the building while you own it and that you are depreciating along with the rest of the building. If you own more than one property you rent out—for example, you rent both your main home and a vacation home—the $1 million limit is applied to each separately.

Annual Expense Limit

You may use the SHST only if the total amount paid during the year for repairs, maintenance, improvements, and similar expenses for a building does not exceed the lesser of $10,000 or 2% of the unadjusted basis of the building.

EXAMPLE: Sam owns a vacation home that he rents part time. It has a $100,000 unadjusted basis—that is, it cost $100,000. He may use the SHST only in those years when the total amount he spends on the building is $2,000 or less (2% x 100,000 = $2,000).

IRS regulations don't address how to calculate basis for purposes of the SHST when you rent only a room or rooms in a home, instead of the entire property. Presumably, your SHST basis should only cover the part of the home you rent. You can calculate this based on the percentage of the home that is rented. Compare the square footage of the entire home with the square footage of the room or rooms you rent out.

EXAMPLE: Sheila owns a three bedroom home and rents one of the bedrooms to short-term guests. Her home cost $200,000 and is 1,000 square feet. The bedroom she rents out is 200 square feet or 20% of the home's total square footage. She determines that her basis for purposes of the SHST is $40,000 (20% x $200,000 = $40,000).

When computing the amount you spend for purposes of the SHST annual limit, you count everything you spent during the year, including amounts that may come within the routine maintenance and de minimis safe harbors discussed below. If you can't use the SHST because the limit is exceeded, you may still use these other safe harbors.

Claiming the SHST

The small taxpayer safe harbor must be claimed anew each year by filing an election with your timely filed tax return, which is due by October 15 (if you obtain an extension of time to file). Thus, you can use the SHST for amounts paid during 2020 by filing the election with your 2020 tax return, which must be filed no later than October 15, 2021.

EXAMPLE: Sam owns a single-family home that he rents out 20% of the year to various short-term guests through Airbnb. It has a $200,000 unadjusted basis (that is, it cost $200,000). During 2020, he paid $200 to a plumber to fix a plumbing problem, fixed a window for $400, and replaced the home's water heater for $2,400. Sam qualifies for the small taxpayer safe harbor because the $3,000 he spent on repairs, improvements, and maintenance during 2020 is less than 2% of his building's unadjusted basis (2% x $200,0000 = $4,000). By filing an election to use the SHST, he may currently deduct 20% of $3,000 on his 2020 IRS Schedule E—which means he gets a $600 deduction. He can do this whether or not any of these expenses, such as the water heater replacement, would be considered an improvement under the regular repair rules discussed below. Those rules do not need to be followed when you fit under the SHST rules.

You can claim the SHST for some years and refrain from doing so for other years—it's entirely up to you. The SHST is also claimed on a building-by-building basis. Thus, if you own more than one short-term rental home or other building, you can claim the SHST for some buildings and not use it for others.

There is no IRS form for this election. However, it is a very simple document you can easily create yourself and attach to your return. You can use the following format:

Section 1.263(a)-3(h) Safe Harbor Election for Small Taxpayers

Taxpayer's name: _____

Taxpayer's address: _____

Taxpayer's identification number: _____

The taxpayer is hereby making the safe harbor election for small taxpayers under Section 1.263(a)-3(h) for the following building property:

_____ [describe] _____.

Once this annual election is made, it may not be revoked for the year it covers.

Routine Maintenance Safe Harbor

The second potentially useful safe harbor for landlords is the routine maintenance safe harbor. (IRS Reg. § 1.263(a)-3(i).) Expenses that qualify as routine maintenance under this provision are deductible in a single year. Unlike with the safe harbor for small taxpayers, there are no annual dollar limits with this safe harbor. However, there are some significant limits on when rental building owners may use this safe harbor.

What Is Routine Maintenance?

Routine maintenance consists of recurring work a building owner does to keep an entire building, or each system in a building, in ordinarily efficient operating condition. Routine maintenance includes two activities:

- inspection, cleaning, and testing of the building structure and each building system, and
- replacement of damaged or worn parts with comparable and commercially available replacement parts.

However, building maintenance qualifies for the routine maintenance safe harbor only if, when you placed the building or building system into service, you reasonably expected to perform such maintenance more than once every ten years. A nonexclusive list of examples of maintenance for rental properties usually performed more than once every ten years includes such items as:

- inspecting, cleaning, and repairing HVAC units
- clearing and replacing rain gutters
- inspecting and replacing sprinklers
- smoke detector inspection and replacement
- lighting inspection and replacement
- paint touch-up
- chimney inspection and cleaning
- furnace inspection, cleaning, and repair, and
- inspecting and replacing washing machine hoses.

The more-than-once-every-ten-years requirement would seem to eliminate use of the routine maintenance safe harbor for building components that typically don't need such frequent maintenance—for example, roofs, windows, and wooden or tile flooring. However, repairs to such components may be currently deductible under the regular IRS repair regulations discussed below.

Adopting the Routine Maintenance Safe Harbor

Unlike the safe harbor for small taxpayers discussed above, the routine maintenance safe harbor is not claimed each year by filing an optional election with your tax return. Rather, the routine maintenance safe harbor is a method of accounting you adopt. Moreover, after you adopt it, you must use it every year. You adopt the routine maintenance safe harbor by currently deducting expenses that come within it on your books and on your tax return. Its use is completely voluntary.

Any expense you deduct under the routine maintenance safe harbor is counted toward your annual limit under the small taxpayer safe harbor. For example, if your annual SHST limit is $5,000 and you deduct $4,000 for maintenance under the routine maintenance safe harbor, you'll only be able to deduct an additional $1,000 under the small taxpayer safe harbor. No amount is deductible under the small taxpayer safe harbor if the annual limit is exceeded. Thus, for example, if your annual SHST limit is $5,000 and you deduct $6,000 under the routine maintenance safe harbor, you won't be entitled to any deduction under the small taxpayer safe harbor. But you can still use the routine maintenance safe harbor, which has no annual limit.

De Minimis Safe Harbor

The third safe harbor is the de minimis safe harbor. (IRS Reg. § 1.263(a)-1(f).) You may use this safe harbor to currently deduct any low-cost items used in your rental activity, regardless of whether or not the item would constitute a repair or an improvement under the regular repair regulations. The safe harbor can be used for personal property and for building components that come within the deduction ceiling.

The maximum amount that can be deducted under this safe harbor is $2,500 per item. Like the SHST, this safe harbor is claimed by filing an election with your annual tax return. You must also adopt an accounting policy requiring such treatment.

As with the routine maintenance safe harbor, all expenses you deduct using the de minimis safe harbor must be counted toward the annual limit for using the safe harbor for small taxpayers (the lesser of 2% of the rental's cost or $10,000). For example, if your annual SHST limit is $2,000, and you deduct $2,500 using the de minimis safe harbor, you may not use the SHST that year. But if you deducted only $1,000 using the de minimis safe harbor, you could deduct an additional $1,000 using the SHST. (See Chapter 7 for a detailed analysis of the de minimis safe harbor.)

Repair Versus Improvement: Analysis Under the Regulations

If you are unable to take advantage of any of the safe harbors described above, you must determine whether the expense involved is for an improvement or a repair by applying the IRS repair regulations. (IRS Reg. § 1.263(a)-3.) The cost of improvements must be depreciated over several years, while repair costs may be currently deducted in a single year.

Under the regulations, an improvement occurs when property undergoes a betterment, adaptation, or restoration. Repairs usually cost less than improvements, but under the IRS regulations, quite large expenditures can qualify as repairs. It all depends on the extent and nature of the change involved. Following is a brief overview of the complex IRS repair regulations. For comprehensive treatment, refer to *Every Landlord's Tax Deduction Guide*, by Stephen Fishman (Nolo). You can also read the voluminous repair regulations on the IRS website at www.irs.gov/irb/2013-43_IRB/ar05.html; the IRS has also created a detailed set of FAQs about them at www.irs.gov/businesses/small-businesses-self-employed/tangible-property-final-regulations.

Betterments

Betterments include expenses for fixing a pre-existing defect or condition, enlarging or expanding your property, or increasing the capacity, strength, or quality of your property. Only material changes to property are betterments that must be depreciated. A material change is one that is significant or important. For example, adding a new bathroom to your home would be a material change. However, punching a hole in a kitchen wall to open up the space between the kitchen and dining room would likely not be viewed as material.

Work you periodically do to refresh your property is not a betterment and need not be depreciated if the refresh consists of cosmetic and layout changes and general repairs and maintenance to keep the unit in ordinarily efficient condition. For example, the cost of painting your home or refinishing the floors need not be depreciated. However, any substantial remodeling you perform during a refresh must be depreciated.

Betterment	Repair
Replace wooden roof shingles with new solar shingles	Replace wooden roof shingles with comparable asphalt roof shingles
Install new insulation throughout home, including attic, walls, and crawlspaces resulting in a 50% reduction in the building's annual energy and power costs	Install new part in furnace that makes it 10% more efficient
Extensive building remodel including replacing large parts of exterior walls with windows, rebuilding interior and exterior facades, replacing vinyl floors with ceramic flooring, replacing ceiling tiles with acoustic tiles, and removing and rebuilding walls to move rooms	Cosmetic and layout changes to building, including patching holes in walls, repainting, replacing damaged ceiling tiles, cleaning and repairing wood flooring, and power washing building exterior

Restorations

Restorations include replacing a substantial structural part of your property, or rebuilding a substantial portion of your property to a like-new condition after it has fallen into disrepair. IRS examples indicate that substantial means replacing or rebuilding at least 30% of the property involved.

Restoration	Repair
Replacing two-thirds (9 out of 12) of the windows in a home	Replacing one out of ten windows in a home
Replacing entire leaking roof that caused structural damage to building	Replacing only the waterproof membrane portion of roof to solve leakage problem—membrane not a significant portion the roof
Replacing all wiring in building's electrical system	Replacing 30% of wiring in building's electrical system

Adaptations

Adaptations include expenses for altering your property to a use that is not consistent with the intended ordinary use of your property when you began renting it. Adaptations aren't terribly common in the context of residential rentals. Examples would include converting a garage or basement into a guest room.

How to Deduct Repairs and Maintenance

Repairs and maintenance expenses are operating expenses that you deduct on IRS Schedule E (see Chapter 10). They are both currently deductible, so whether an expense is classified as a repair or maintenance makes no practical difference to your bottom line. However, you are required to list each type of expense separately in Schedule E. As a result, you must track them separately throughout the year. The cost includes what you spend on materials, parts, and labor. If you do the work yourself, you don't get a deduction for the value of your own labor.

> EXAMPLE: Kim rents her Seattle home to short-term guests while she's out of town. One of Kim's guests complains that the fan in the bathroom is making a funny noise. Kim hires Andy, a handyman, to repair the fan. Andy finds that the fan just needs to be cleaned. He does so, and charges Kim $50, which she pays. Kim may add the $50 to the expenses she lists in her Schedule E for the year. If instead of hiring Andy, Kim cleans the fan herself, the value of her labor does not count as deductible maintenance. Kim spent nothing for materials or parts, so she gets no deduction for repairing the fan herself.

When Guests Pay for Repairs

If you are forced to do a repair because of damage caused by a guest, you may deduct the cost from the guest's security deposit or charge the guest an extra fee for the repair. A security deposit does not constitute taxable income. However, if you keep all or part of a security deposit because a guest has caused damage, that amount is taxable income. When you fix the damage, the amount spent on the repair is a deductible expense that will offset the additional income.

> EXAMPLE: Ed rents his Park City, Utah, vacation home to short-term guests. One of his guests informs him that he accidentally broke a window with one of his skis. He hires a repairman to fix the window at a cost of $100 and deducts the amount from the guest's $500 security deposit. He refunds the remaining $400 to the guest. The $100 Ed kept is rental income he must report on his Schedule E for the year. But the $100 he spent to fix the window is an expense he can deduct that year. This offsets the $100 he kept, so he ends up paying no tax on the amount.

If you deduct money from a guest's deposit for damage and don't fix it, you'll have no expense deduction to offset the increased rental income.

Properly Document Repairs

Good documentation is the key to winning any argument with the IRS. Here are some tips for properly documenting your repairs:

- **Get an invoice for every repair.** Make sure it describes the work in a way that is consistent with a repair, not an improvement. Good words to use include repair, fix, patch, mend, redo, recondition, and restore. An invoice should not include any words that indicate an improvement—for example improvement, replacement, remodel, renovation, addition, construction, rehab, upgrade, or new. Of course, your invoice will not, by itself, establish whether something is a repair or an improvement— the facts must be consistent with what the invoice says.

- **Make sure your repairs are classified as such in all your books and accounting records.** This problem can easily crop up if you have a bookkeeper or accountant do your books—who may list a repair as a capital improvement. If an IRS auditor sees this, it will be curtains for your repair deduction.

- **If you're doing an extensive repair, take before-and-after photographs** to show the extent of the work and that the property has not been made substantially more valuable. ⬤

Deducting Long-Term Assets

Long-term assets are property that lasts more than one year—for example, buildings, tangible personal property like stoves and refrigerators, and furniture. In tax parlance, such long-term property is called a capital asset because it is part of your capital investment in your short-term rental business or investment activity. Special tax rules apply to deducting long-term assets. Real property must be deducted a little at a time over many years using a process called depreciation. However, personal property and many land improvements can often be deducted in a single year.

You can only take depreciation deductions for property that you own. Thus, you get no real property depreciation deduction if you're a tenant who subleases his or her rental unit to short-term guests. Instead, you may deduct a portion of your rent (see Chapter 9). However, you may be able to depreciate furniture and other personal property items you own and use in your rental activity.

If you own the property you rent, depreciation may be one of your largest deductions. Many rental property owners simply have their accountants handle their depreciation and never bother to learn much about it. However, it's worth your time and trouble to understand it in some detail. This will enable you to:

- make sure your accountant determines your depreciation deductions properly—depreciation is not as cut and dried as you might think, and the way your accountant figures your depreciation may not be the best way, and
- figure your depreciation deduction yourself if you choose to prepare your own tax returns.

CAUTION

Depreciation is not optional. Unlike all the other tax deductions discussed in this book, depreciation is not optional. You *must* take a depreciation deduction if you qualify for it. If you fail to take it, the IRS will treat you as if you had taken it. This means that when you sell your property, its basis (value for tax purposes) will be reduced by the amount of depreciation you failed to claim. As a result, you'll have a larger profit from the sale that you'll have to pay taxes on.

Depreciating Property Used in Your Rental Activity

You depreciate both real and personal property that you use in your rental activity. The real property component of your depreciation deduction consists of the building (or portion of a building) that you rent to short-term guests—whether a single-family home, duplex, condo, vacation home, mobile home, or other property. Your real property includes the building structure and all its components, including walls, floors, ceilings, windows, doors, plumbing fixtures (such as sinks and bathtubs), pipes, ducts, bathroom fixtures, stairs, fire escapes, electrical wiring, lighting fixtures, chimneys, air conditioning and heating systems, and other parts that form the structure. You may also deduct land improvements, such as driveways, fences, and swimming pools, along with the building; however, you also have the option to deduct these separately (see below). Land itself cannot be depreciated because it never wears out and is not considered part of the building for depreciation purposes.

Personal property includes furniture, appliances, lawnmowers, and other movable tangible property. Since it doesn't last as long as real property, personal property is depreciated over far fewer years than real property. Moreover, special tax rules may allow you to deduct the cost of personal property items in a single year.

You can begin to take depreciation for any real or personal property you use in your rental activity as soon as you place your rental property in service. This occurs when you list your property on a short-term rental platform like Airbnb or otherwise make it available for short-term rental. You don't have to actually rent the property to place it into service in your rental activity—it just has to be available for rent. You can no longer take depreciation deductions for your rental property when you cease offering the property for rent, or you sell or otherwise transfer ownership of the property or the depreciation period ends (which can take years).

Since you're renting out your property part time, you must prorate your deductions based on the percentage of the time the property is used for rental versus personal use. If you rent a room or rooms in your home instead of the entire home, you must also prorate your real property depreciation deduction based on the amount of space that is rented. (See Chapter 9).

How to Depreciate Real Property

At its core, depreciation is simple: You figure out how much the property you want to depreciate is worth for tax purposes (the property's basis), how long the IRS says you must depreciate it for (its recovery period), and then you deduct a certain percentage of its basis each year during its recovery period. Land itself is not depreciated, since it lasts forever.

Determining Your Property's Basis

How much you can depreciate each year depends, first and foremost, on how much your property is worth for tax purposes—this is called basis in tax lingo. The larger your basis, the larger your depreciation deductions will be. Short-term rental hosts typically live in their property for some time before they convert it to a part-time rental property. When you convert property from personal use to rental use, your basis is the *lesser* of the following values on the date you place the property into service in your rental activity:

- the property's fair market value, or
- your adjusted basis.

If you rent a room or rooms in your home, instead of the entire home, figure your basis for your entire property and then prorate the amount you can depreciate according to the percentage of the home you rent. (See Chapter 9.)

Fair market value. Fair market value is the price at which the property would change hands between a buyer and a seller, neither under undue pressure to buy or sell, and both having reasonable knowledge of all the relevant facts. Sales of similar property in the area are helpful in figuring out the fair market value of the property. You may also elect to have the property's value appraised as of the date of its conversion to rental property.

Adjusted basis. If, like most hosts, you purchased the property and you're now offering the property or part of the property (like a room in your home) for short-term rent, your adjusted basis is equal to:

- the purchase price (less the cost of your land), plus
- certain facilitative expenses—for example, appraisal fees, escrow fees, title search, recording fees, legal costs, and other fees paid to purchase the property, plus
- the cost of permanent additions or improvements you made to the property—for example, the cost of adding a new bathroom or roof (see "Depreciating Improvements After Rental Activity Begins," below), and
- prorated, if applicable, by the percentage of space that is rented.

Because you can't depreciate land, you must deduct the value of the land from the purchase price to figure your basis. There are various ways to calculate the value of your land: You can use the relative values shown on your property tax bill, determine the replacement cost of your building and improvements with an appraisal or by calculating the cost yourself, or use records of comparable land sales. For a highly detailed discussion of how to determine the relative values of land and buildings, see Chapter 6 of *Every Landlord's Tax Deduction Guide*, by Stephen Fishman (Nolo).

The cost of any repairs you make to the building before it's offered for rent are not deductible or added to basis. For example, if, before listing your home as a short-term rental, you paid to repair the furnace, the cost is not deductible or added to basis. The only exception to this rule is where repairs qualify as start-up expenses for a brand new rental business. This is a limited deduction of up to $5,000 you may take for getting a new rental business up and going (see Chapter 5).

Ordinarily, your adjusted basis will be lower than the fair market value because residential real estate usually appreciates in value each year.

EXAMPLE: John purchased his home ten years ago for $140,000. Based on the value in his property tax bill, he figures the land was worth $14,000. Before he started renting the home to short-term guests last year, he added $28,000 of permanent improvements, including a new roof and an additional bathroom. Because land is not depreciable, John only includes the cost of the house and improvements when figuring his adjusted basis for depreciation—$168,000 ($140,000 + $28,000). When John first listed his house on Airbnb it had a fair market value of $250,000. John must use his adjusted basis of $168,000 as the basis for depreciation on the house because it is less than the fair market value on the date of the conversion to rental use. If John only rented a room in his home that was 10% of the total square footage, then his depreciable basis would be $16,800 (10% x $168,000 = $16,800).

How Long Is the Depreciation Period?

The tax law assigns a certain amount of time—called the recovery period—over which all long-term assets must be depreciated. Real property has the longest recovery period. The period for residential real property is 27.5 years. The period for nonresidential real property—that is, commercial property—is 39 years. Unfortunately, if you rent primarily to short-term guests, it could be classified as commercial property instead of residential property for depreciation purposes. That means your annual depreciation deductions will be 29.5% smaller because you must depreciate over 39 years instead of 27.5 years.

A dwelling unit must be classified as commercial property, not residential property, if it is occupied on a transient basis. (I.R.C. § 168(e)(2)(A)(ii)(I).) This rule applies to hotels and motels, but it can apply to short-term home rentals as well. It all depends on what transient basis means. Unfortunately, the IRS has provided little guidance. The best guess is that a home or another dwelling is used on a transient basis if over half of the rental use for the year is by a tenant or series of tenants who occupy the unit for less than 30 days per rental. This interpretation is based on old IRS regulations that have been withdrawn but that the IRS says still remain informative. (IRS Reg. §§ 1.167(k)-3(c)(1) and (2) (removed in 1993).)

Under this interpretation of the rules, many hosts who rent to short-term guests would need to classify their property as commercial property for depreciation purposes. It's likely that few hosts are aware of this. It's also unclear if the IRS will actually enforce this interpretation against short-term hosts. However, the safest course is to follow this interpretation if it applies to you. Since it results in a smaller depreciation deduction each year, the IRS will never complain if you do so. If you'd prefer to use the shorter depreciation period to obtain a larger annual deduction, you should discuss the matter with your tax adviser.

EXAMPLE: During one recent year, Max rents his Chicago condominium through Airbnb to 40 different guests for a total of 180 days. None of the guests stays over 14 days. He used the condominium himself for only 60 days during the year. Since more than 50% of the total days of use is transient, the condominium is rented on a transient basis and should be classified as a commercial building for depreciation purposes. This means Max would depreciate the condo over 39 years instead of 27.5 years. The unit has a $200,000 depreciable basis; so he can claim only $5,128 in depreciation. Had the 27.5-year depreciation period for residential property been applicable, he could have claimed $7,272 in depreciation for the year.

How Much to Depreciate Each Year

You use the straight-line method to depreciate real property. With this method you deduct an equal amount of the property's basis each year, except for the first and last years. If your property qualifies as residential property, you deduct 1/27 (3.636%) of its depreciable basis each year. If your property is classified as commercial property, you deduct 1/39 (2.564%) of its basis each year. Your depreciation deduction for the first and last year depends on what month of the year you placed your property into service in your rental activity. For example, if your property's basis is $100,000 and it is classified as commercial property, your maximum depreciation deduction would be $2,564 per year, except for the first and last years. If it is classified as residential property, your annual deduction would be $3,636. You can easily calculate your annual depreciation deduction with accounting and tax preparation software, online calculators, or by using the charts in IRS Publication 946, *How to Depreciate Property*.

However, because short-term hosts don't rent their property full time, they must allocate their depreciation deduction according to how much of the year they do rent the property.

> **EXAMPLE:** Leslie's home has a $100,000 basis and must be depreciated over 39 years. This year, she lived in the home for nine months and rented out to various short-term guests through Airbnb for a total of three months. She gets to claim three months of depreciation for the home. Her depreciation deduction for the year is $100,000 x .03636 x 3/12 = $909.

If you rent a room or rooms in your home, instead of the entire home, your depreciation deduction must be further reduced according to the size of the room or rooms. See Chapter 9 for detailed guidance on how to calculate and allocate your deductions for short-term rentals.

Depreciating Improvements After Rental Activity Begins

Improvements you make to your property after your rental activity begins must be separately depreciated from the original building itself. A building addition or improvement is a material change you make to the building or its various structural components including walls, floors, ceilings, windows, doors, plumbing fixtures (such as sinks and bathtubs), pipes, ducts, bathroom fixtures, stairs, fire escapes, electrical wiring, lighting fixtures, chimneys, and air-conditioning and heating systems. An improvement makes the building or structural component much better than it was before (a betterment), restores it to operating condition after it has fallen into disrepair (a restoration), or adapts it to a new use (an adaptation). Improvements include, but are not limited to, adding or replacing all of the following:

- **Additions**. New bedroom, bathroom, deck, garage, porch, or patio
- **Plumbing**. Septic system, water heater, soft water system, filtration system
- **Heating and air-conditioning**. Heating system, central air-conditioning, furnace, duct work, central humidifier
- **Insulation**. Attic, floors, walls, pipes, duct work
- **Miscellaneous**. Storm windows, door, new roof, central vacuum, wiring upgrades, satellite dish, security system, and
- **Land improvements**. Fences, outdoor lighting, swimming pools, driveways, paved parking areas and other pavements, sidewalks and walkways, sprinkler systems, drainage facilities, and new land-scaping if it will have to be replaced when the building is replaced.

Regular Depreciation

You can always use regular depreciation to deduct the cost of any real property improvement. Start to depreciate an improvement to a building when it is placed in service—that is, when it is ready for use in your rental activity. Depreciate the amount that an addition or improvement costs, including any amount you borrowed to make the addition or improvement. This includes all direct costs, such as material and labor, but not your own labor. If the improvement is to the building structure or structural components, depreciate it over 27.5 or 39 years, using the same method used for the original building as described above. Land improvements are depreciated over 15 years.

If you rent a room or rooms in your home, instead of the entire home, you may take a depreciation deduction for improvements that benefit the entire home, such as a new roof or heating system. The deduction must be prorated according to the percentage of the home that is rented. You may also take depreciation for improvements just for the room or rooms that are rented—for example, a new window for a rental room. In this event, you prorate your deduction according to the amount of time you rent the room.

However, the IRS says you get no deduction for improvements to specific areas of the home that are not rented. For example, you get no deduction for adding a new storm window in a bedroom you do not rent out.

You must keep separate accounts for depreciable additions or improvements made after you place your rental property in service. You add the cost of depreciable additions and improvements to the adjusted basis of your property, which will reduce your tax liability when you sell the property.

In contrast to improvements, the cost of repairs to real property are currently deductible in the year they are made and need not be depreciated. See Chapter 6 for a detailed discussion of how to tell the difference between repairs and improvements.

De Minimis Safe Harbor

Building components that cost $2,500 or less may be deducted in a single year with the de minimis safe harbor deduction. For example, a bathroom sink is a building component. If you spend $2,000 to replace a bathroom sink, the full amount of your depreciable basis can be deducted that year with the de minimis safe harbor deduction instead of being depreciated over five years. Your depreciable basis is the property's cost multiplied by the rental use percentage. Thus, if you rent your home 25% of the time, you could deduct $500 of the cost of a $2,000 bathroom sink. See "De Minimis Safe Harbor," below.

Section 179

Section 179 may only be used by short-term hosts who rent their property over 51% of the time. In other words, if you personally use the property 50% or more of the time, you can't use Section 179. The same property can be deducted with bonus depreciation or the de minimis safe harbor. However, the Tax Cuts and Jobs Act has made Section 179 newly relevant for some short-term hosts. Section 179 can be used to fully deduct in one year up to $1,040,000 (2020) of the cost of the following improvements to nonresidential real property placed in service after the property was first placed in service:

- roofs
- heating, ventilation, and air-conditioning property
- fire protection and alarm systems, and
- security systems. (I.R.C. § 179(e)(2).)

Bonus Depreciation

Bonus depreciation is mostly used to deduct personal property, as discussed below. However, you have the option of deducting 100% of land improvements using bonus depreciation for land improvements placed into service during September 9, 2017 through December 31, 2022.

Improvements that Are Qualified Improvement Property

The Tax Cuts and Jobs Act established a new category of depreciable real property starting in 2018: "qualified improvement property." Such property consists of improvements to the interior of *nonresidential* real property after it has been placed into service in business. However, it does not include improvements related to the enlargement of a building, an elevator or escalator, or the internal structural framework of a building.

Can improvements to a short-term rental be qualified improvement property? Yes! As discussed above (see "How Long Is the Depreciation Period?"), a residence used for short-term rentals is considered nonresidential property for tax purposes if the guests occupy it on a transient basis. In this event, the original property is depreciated over 39 years instead of 27.5 years. Qualified improvement property is depreciated over 15 years.

If you classify your property as nonresidential property, improvements you make after you place the property in service in your rental activity can qualify as qualified improvement property. This is generally advantageous tax-wise. Taxpayers who have qualified improvement property may deduct the cost one of three ways:

- fully deduct the cost in one year with 100% bonus depreciation
- deduct the cost with Section 179 expensing, subject to a $1,040,000 annual limit for 2020 (provided the property is rented over 50% of the time), or
- depreciate the cost over 15 years using straight-line deprecation.
- Using bonus depreciation can provide a substantial deduction that can result in a net operating loss (NOL) for the year, depending on the taxpayer's other income and expenses. NOLs for 2018 through 2020 may be carried back five years (deducted against income for those years) resulting in a tax refund for one or more of those years.

EXAMPLE: Arthur owns a vacation home that he starts to rent out to short-term guests on March 1, 2019. He rents the property 75% of the time and lives in it 25% of the year. Because his guests occupy the home on a transient basis, he classified the home as nonresidential property to be depreciated over a 39-year term. In 2020, he remodels the home by taking out several of the interior (nonstructural) walls to create a large open space. He uses 100% bonus depreciation to fully deduct 75% of the cost in 2020. This results in a $20,000 NOL for 2020. He applies this NOL to his 2015 through 2019 taxes, resulting in a tax refund.

When Congress wrote the Tax Cuts and Jobs Act, it intended to permit qualified improvement property to be fully deducted in one year using 100% bonus depreciation or depreciated over 15 years. However, due to a drafting error, this provision was left out of the TCJA. This error was corrected when Congress enacted the CARES Act in 2020, retroactive to 2018. The 100% bonus depreciation and 15-year depreciation fixes are retroactive to 2018. Hosts who are depreciating qualified improvement property placed in service during 2018 or 2019 over 39 years, must correct their depreciation deductions for those years. This is not optional. They may now use bonus depreciation (or Section 179 where applicable) to fully deduct the cost of the improvements in one year. Alternatively, they may elect out of bonus depreciation and depreciate the improvements over 15 years instead of 39.

Hosts who have filed two or more annual returns depreciating 2018 or 2019 qualified improvement property over 39 years must file IRS Form 3115, *Application for Change in Accounting Method*, with their current-year tax return to correct the recovery period. Hosts who have only filed one annual return with the 39-year period may file an amended return for that prior year or may file Form 3115 with their current year return. The Form 3115 or amended return will show (1) the adjustments required if the taxpayer had claimed 100% bonus depreciation for the improvements, or (2) elect out of bonus depreciation and show the adjustments to depreciate the property over 15 years. It's wise to have a tax professional to prepare these forms. Hosts who used Section 179 to fully deduct qualified improvement property for 2018 or 2019 don't have to do anything.

When You Sell Your Property

Every year, you must decrease your property's basis by the amount of depreciation you took, or should have taken, on the property. However, if the amount of depreciation you're allowed to deduct for the year is limited by the vacation home rules covered in Chapter 3, you need only reduce your basis by the allowed amount, if any.

Reductions in your property's basis increase the taxable profit you earn if you sell the property, since your profit is determined by subtracting your adjusted basis from the sales price. The amount of any profit on the sale attributable to the depreciation deductions you took in prior years is taxed at a single 25% rate (however, if your top tax rate is below 25%, the lower rate applies). Thus, when you sell your property, you effectively give back the depreciation deductions you took on it. However, in the meantime your annual taxes have been lowered by these annual deductions. In effect, depreciation allows you to defer payment of tax on your rental income from the years in which it was earned to the year it is sold. Moreover, if you never sell the property you'll never have to pay the 25% tax.

Personal Property

Personal property is any long-term asset that is not real property. It includes anything that is not part of the building structure itself, a structural component, or land improvement. Personal property is movable, or at least removable, from the building itself without causing permanent damage. Because it usually costs much less than real property and lasts far less long, different rules apply to deducting personal property you use in your rental activity.

The following types of items inside your home, vacation home, or other property you rent short-term are personal property:

- furniture
- refrigerators, stoves, dishwashers, microwaves, and other kitchen appliances
- carpeting that is tacked down (but not glued down)
- drapes, curtains, and window blinds
- washers and dryers
- fire extinguishers and fire alarms
- plants inside your home
- portable window air conditioners and space heaters
- movable and removable partitions, and
- televisions.

Personal property also includes items you use in your rental activity but aren't used by your guests—for example, vehicles, lawn mowers and other landscaping and maintenance equipment, computers, cellphones, and office furniture. Such property is deductible the same as personal property inside the dwelling. However, you may claim a separate depreciation deduction for your automobile only if you use the actual expense method to figure your deduction instead of the standard mileage rate (see Chapter 5).

No Deductions for Personal Property in Common Areas

If you rent a room or rooms in your home, instead of your entire home, the IRS takes the position that you can only deduct personal property located in the room or rooms you rent to short-term guests. For example, if you rent a bedroom to short-term guests, you may deduct the cost of purchasing new furniture for the bedroom or converting old furniture to rental use. But you may not deduct property used in common areas such as your kitchen or living room, even if your guests use it. For example, you couldn't deduct the cost of a dining room table in your kitchen, even though your short-term guests use it while they stay in your home.

Special rules may apply that allow you to deduct the cost of personal property in a single year, rather than having to depreciate the cost over several years. However, the rules differ depending on whether you purchase personal property specifically for rental use, or you convert property you already own for your rental activity. If you purchase property for your rental activity—that is, you don't use it personally first—you can usually deduct the cost in one year using one of the following tax rules:

- the de minimis safe harbor
- material and supplies deduction
- 100% bonus depreciation, or
- Section 179 expensing.

If none of these rules apply, you'll have to deduct the property over several years (usually five) using regular depreciation. You'll also have to use regular depreciation to deduct the cost of personal property you convert to rental use.

De Minimis Safe Harbor

IRS repair regulations that went into effect in 2014 created the de minimis safe harbor deduction. (IRS Reg. § 1.263(a)-1(f).) You can use the deminimis safe harbor to currently deduct the cost of personal property you buy to use in your rental activity that costs up to $2,500 per item. This can result in a substantial deduction since there is no limit on the number of items costing up to $2,500 you can deduct each year. The de minimis safe harbor is optional, but you should elect to use it if you want to deduct as much personal property as you can in the year you buy the property for your rental activity.

What Can Be Deducted

If you elect to use the de minimis safe harbor, you deduct in a single year all tangible personal property you purchase for your rental activity whose cost falls within the $2,500 limit described below. You may also deduct spare parts to repair or maintain personal property. Fortunately for short-term rental hosts, you can use the de minimis safe harbor to deduct the cost of property even if you don't use it 100% of the time for your rental activity. That means you can deduct property that is located in common areas like your kitchen or living room if you allow rental guests to use those areas. However, your deduction is limited to the dollar amount of your rental use percentage.

> **EXAMPLE:** Sheila rents out her vacation home 25% of the time. She purchases a $2,000 sofa for the living room that qualifies for the de minimis safe harbor. She may deduct 25% of the cost in one year using the de minimis safe harbor, so she gets a $500 deduction.

If you elect to use the de minimis safe harbor, you must also apply it to all items you buy during the year for your rental activity with an economic useful life of 12 months or less whose cost is within the de minimis limit. The economic useful life of property is the period it may reasonably be expected to be useful to the taxpayer.

> **EXAMPLE:** During the year, Sheila from the above example spends $500 for perishable food she supplies to her short-term guests. The food has a useful life of less than 12 months. Sheila should currently deduct the cost under the de minimis safe harbor.

De Minimis Safe Harbor Versus Bonus Depreciation

As a result of the Tax Cuts and Jobs Act, you can fully deduct much of the same expenses in a single year using 100% bonus depreciation (through 2022) as you can deduct using the de minimis safe harbor. However, the advantage of the de minimis safe harbor is its simplicity. All expenses deducted with the safe harbor are currently deducted as business operating expenses. You may deduct them as "other" expenses on your Schedule E. You can list the total amount as "de minimis safe harbor expenses." Unlike with bonus depreciation, you don't need to list your safe harbor expenses on IRS Form 4562, *Depreciation and Amortization (Including Information on Listed Property)*. Nor do you have to create or maintain depreciation schedules for property items or include them in your accounting records as assets. Also, bonus depreciation may only be used to deduct personal property, not building components like a bathroom sink that can be deducted with the safe harbor.

The big advantage of bonus depreciation is that it is not subject to a $2,500 per item ceiling. You can use the de minimis safe harbor to deduct items costing $2,500 or less and use bonus depreciation to deduct more expensive personal property items. Another potential advantage is that using bonus depreciation does not adversely affect the pass-through tax deduction (see Chapter 8). At certain income levels, this deduction is based on the value of the depreciable property used in your rental activity. Property deducted with the de minimis safe harbor does not count for this purpose; so, theoretically, using the safe harbor could reduce your pass-through deduction. However, the amount of property involved for most hosts is likely so small there would not be much of a practical difference.

Components acquired to repair or improve a unit of tangible property are also deducted under the de minimis safe harbor if they fall within the $2,500 limit. This can include building components.

EXAMPLE: Larry pays $2,000 for a bathroom sink for his vacation home that he rents to short-term guests 25% of the year. The new sink is an improvement to a unit of property—the building's plumbing system. Ordinarily, it would have to be depreciated (it may not be deducted with bonus depreciation or Section 179 because it's a building component, not personal property). However, because its cost is within the $2,500 de minimis limit, Larry may deduct it in one year using the de minimis safe harbor.

Maximum De Minimis Amount

You may use the de minimis safe harbor only for property whose cost does not exceed $2,500 per invoice, or $2,500 per item as substantiated by the invoice. You must include delivery and installation charges listed on the invoice. If the cost exceeds $2,500 per invoice (or item), no part of the item's cost may be deducted using the de minimis safe harbor. To determine whether the cost of an item falls within the $2,500 limit, you must apply the full invoice amount, even if you use the item only part time for your rental activity and therefore would be allowed to deduct only part of the full invoice amount.

> EXAMPLE: Dave purchases a $3,000 HVAC unit for his home that he rents 25% of the time. He may not deduct any part of the cost using the de minimis safe harbor because the cost of the unit exceeds the $2,500 ceiling. This is true even though Dave's deduction would have been limited to $750 (25% rental use x $3,000 invoice amount = $750 deduction).

Claiming the De Minimis Safe Harbor

To claim the de minimis safe harbor, you must file an election with your tax return each year using the following format:

Section 1.263(a)-1(f) De Minimis Safe Harbor Election

Taxpayer's name: _____

Taxpayer's address: _____

Taxpayer's identification number: _____

The taxpayer is hereby making the de minimis safe harbor election under Section 1.263(a)-1(f).

When you make this election, it applies to all expenses you incur that qualify for the de minimis safe harbor. You cannot pick and choose which items you want to include. You must also include items that would otherwise be deductible as materials and supplies. You must also currently deduct all these items in your accounting records.

Materials and Supplies Deduction

"Materials and supplies" are tangible property used or consumed in your rental activity that fall within any of the following categories:

- any item of tangible personal property that cost $200 or less
- any item of personal property with an economic useful life of 12 months or less, or
- components acquired to maintain or repair tangible property—that is, spare parts. (I.R.C. § 1.162-3.)

The cost of such items may be deducted in the year the item is used or consumed in your rental activity—which may be later than the year purchased. To use this deduction, you are supposed to keep records of when the items are used or consumed in your rental activity—something few small landlords do in practice. For this reason, this deduction will be useless for most hosts. Fortunately, they can use the de minimis safe harbor discussed above instead to deduct materials and supplies.

Incidental Materials and Supplies

Incidental materials and supplies are personal property items that are carried on hand and for which no record of consumption is kept or for which beginning and ending inventories are not taken. (IRS Reg. § 1.162-3(a)(2).) In other words, these are inexpensive items not worth keeping track of. Costs of incidental materials and supplies are deductible in the year they are paid for, not when the items are used or consumed in your rental activity.

> EXAMPLE: John purchases one dozen light bulbs he plans to use as replacements for the bulbs in the vacation home he rents part time to short-term guests. The cost was minimal and he does not keep an inventory of each bulb. These are incidental and deductible in the year he paid for them.

Interaction With De Minimis Safe Harbor

If you elect to use the de minimis safe harbor discussed above, you must apply it to amounts paid for all materials and supplies that meet the requirements for deduction under the safe harbor. (IRS Reg. § 1.263(a)-1(f)(3)(ii).) Thus, if you use the de minimis safe harbor, you can largely ignore the materials and supplies deduction. This is to your advantage since the de minimis safe harbor has a $2,500 limit, as opposed to the $200 materials and supplies limit. Moreover, the de minimis safe harbor permits you to deduct the cost of items in the year they are purchased, instead of when they are actually used or consumed in your rental business.

Bonus Depreciation

Bonus depreciation enables you to deduct a substantial percentage of a long-term asset's cost in a single year, instead of depreciating the full cost over many years. As a result of the Tax Cuts and Jobs Act, you can use bonus depreciation to deduct 100% of the cost of qualifying property you purchase and place in service in your short-term rental activity during September 28, 2017 through December 31, 2022. Unlike the de minimis safe harbor, there is no dollar limit on the items you can deduct with bonus depreciation.

Bonus depreciation generally may not be used for real property—for example, you may not use it to deduct the cost of a building. However, it can be used to deduct qualified improvement property. This consists of improvements to the interior of nonresidential real property after it has been placed into service. (See "Improvements that Are Qualified Improvement Property," above.)

You may use bonus depreciation to fully deduct in one year the cost of new or used personal property—for example:

- appliances
- furniture
- office furniture and equipment used in your home office

- removable flooring and carpeting
- cabinets and counters
- wall paneling, and
- decorative and track lighting.

Bonus depreciation may also be used to deduct depreciable land improvements such as swimming pools, sidewalks, fences, landscaping, hot tubs, and driveways.

Bonus depreciation is optional—you don't have to take it if you don't want to. If you don't want to take it, you must inform the IRS as described below. But if you want to get the largest depreciation deduction you can, you'll want to take advantage of the bonus.

You can apply bonus depreciation for assets you use part of the time in your short-term rental activity and use personally the rest of the time. But you must adjust your depreciable basis accordingly. For example, if you rent out a bedroom to short-term guests 25% of the year, you may use bonus depreciation to fully deduct in one year 25% of the cost of a bed you purchase for the room.

> EXAMPLE: Lisa purchases a $4,000 stove for her home in 2020, which she rents to short-term guests 25% of the time. The stove qualifies for 100% bonus depreciation, thus she may deduct in one year 100% of her depreciable basis, which is $1,000 (25% rental use x $4,000 = $1,000). The stove did not qualify for the de minimis safe harbor because it cost more than $2,500.

Property That Qualifies for Bonus Depreciation

You can use bonus depreciation to deduct all types of tangible personal property and off-the-shelf software used for your short-term rental activity. It may be used for cars you use for your rental business, but only if you use the actual expense method to deduct your expenses and use the car at least 51% for business—a maximum of $8,000 may be deducted for a car with bonus depreciation.

The property may be used or new, but you must not have used it before acquiring it. Thus, you can't convert property you previously used for personal use to rental use and deduct the cost with bonus depreciation. You can use bonus depreciation only for property that you purchase—not for leased property or property you inherit or receive as a gift. You also can't use it for property that you buy from a relative or a corporation or an organization that you control. Only property that is placed in service during the tax year qualifies, meaning the property is ready and available for use (even if it is never actually used).

Bonus depreciation can't be used for:
- land
- buildings or building structural components (except for qualified improvement property)
- intangible property, such as patents, copyrights, and trademarks, or
- property outside the United States.

Bonus Depreciation Applies Class-Wide

If you use bonus depreciation, you must use it for all assets you purchase and place in service during the year that fall within the same class. An asset class consists of the assets that are deducted over the same period of time using regular depreciation. Personal property used by your short-term guests is depreciated over five years. This includes appliances, carpeting, and furniture. Computers and cars are also five-year property. Office equipment is seven-year property. Thus, for example, if you buy a new bed for your short-term rental activity and take bonus depreciation, you must take bonus depreciation for all other personal property you purchase that year for your activity, including refrigerators, chairs, stoves, carpeting, and dishwashers.

If you want to pick and choose which personal property items to deduct in one year, and which to depreciate, you should use Section 179 instead of bonus depreciation (see below).

Calculating the Bonus Amount

You figure your bonus depreciation deduction by multiplying the depreciable basis of the asset by the applicable bonus percentage. An asset's basis is its initial cost, plus sales tax, delivery, and installation charges. It doesn't matter if you pay cash or finance the purchase with a credit card or bank loan. However, if you pay for property with both cash and a trade-in, bonus depreciation may only be applied to the cash paid, not the trade-in.

As shown in the following chart, the percentages vary depending on when the property was placed in service in your short-term rental activity. The bonus percentage is 100% for property purchased and placed in service during September 28, 2017 through December 31, 2022. Thus, the full cost of qualifying property can be deducted for the next five years.

Year Property Placed In Service	Bonus Depreciation Percentage
1/1/2015 through 9/27/2017 (new property only)	50%
9/27/2017 through 2022	100%
2023	80%
2024	60%
2025	40%
2026	20%
2027 and later	0%

Property acquired before September 28, 2017 is subject to a 50% bonus depreciation rate if it was placed in service in 2017, 40% if placed in service in 2018, 30% if placed in service in 2019, and 0 if placed in service after 2019.

There are no dollar limits on the total bonus depreciation deduction you may take each year. You may take your full deduction even if it exceeds your income for the year resulting in a net operating loss.

Opting Out of the Bonus

Bonus depreciation is applied automatically to all taxpayers who qualify for it. However, the deduction is always optional. You need not take it if you don't want to. To opt out, you must file Form 4562, *Depreciation and Amortization (Including Information on Listed Property)*. The form's instructions explain how to opt out. In addition, most tax preparation software has a box you can check to opt out of bonus depreciation. It may be advantageous to opt out if you expect your income to go up substantially in future years, placing you in a higher tax bracket; or if bonus depreciation will result in losses you're unable to deduct because of the passive loss rules (see Chapter 11).

CAUTION

When you opt out, you do so for the entire class of assets. It's very important to understand that if you opt out of the bonus, you must do so for the entire class of assets, not just one asset within a class. This is the same rule that applies when you decide to take the bonus.

Section 179 Expensing

Section 179 of the tax code is similar to bonus depreciation in that it allows a business owner to deduct in one year the full cost of personal property used in business. However, deductions under Section 179 are subject to so many restrictions that they are unavailable to many short-term rental hosts.

The most significant restriction is that Section 179 can only be used to deduct property that is used in your short-term rental business over 50% of the time. Thus, if you personally use the property over 50% of the time, you may not deduct it with Section 179. This eliminates the majority of short-term hosts from being able to use Section 179.

EXAMPLE: Felix owns a vacation home he lives in three months per year and rents to short-term guests through Airbnb for a total of one month. The home is vacant the rest of the time; thus, it is used 25% for the rental activity. Felix purchased a $4,000 sofa for the home that he would like to fully deduct using Section 179. It isn't eligible though because the sofa (and everything else in the vacation home) is only used 25% of the time in Felix's rental activity.

Even if the 51% rental use requirement is satisfied, there are other restrictions on using Section 179:

- If your rental use of property you deducted with Section 179 falls below 51% during the depreciation period (five years for most personal property), you have to pay back your Section 179 deduction to the IRS—a process called recapture.
- You can't use Section 179 to deduct more in one year than your net taxable business income for the year (not counting the Section 179 deduction, but including your spouse's salary and business income). Undeductible amounts are carried forward to be deducted in future years. Thus, Section 179 may never result in a loss.
- Section 179 can only be used if your short-term rental activity qualifies as a business for tax purposes.
- There is an annual limit on the amount of property that can be deducted with Section 179. For 2020, the limit is $1,040,000. This limit should affect few hosts.
- For 2017 and earlier, Section 179 couldn't be used to deduct personal property used in residential rental buildings. The Tax Cuts and Jobs Act eliminated this prohibition for 2018 and later.

Bonus depreciation and the de minimis safe harbor are subject to none of these restrictions. However, Section 179 has one potential advantage over bonus depreciation: Unlike bonus depreciation, which must apply to all assets in the same class, you can pick and choose which assets to deduct with Section 179 and which to deduct using regular depreciation. This enables you to target your deductions to get the "right" amount of income you want for the year.

Regular Depreciation

If you purchase an item of personal property for your rental activity that you can't deduct fully in one year using the rules described above, you'll have to depreciate the cost over several years. Depreciation for personal property works much the same as for real property. You determine:

- the property's basis—normally the cost of new or used property you purchase for use in your rental activity after you list your property for short-term rental or the fair market value of property you convert to rental use—prorated, if applicable, by the percentage of rental use
- the recovery period—normally five years for personal property, and
- the depreciation method—typically, you can use accelerated depreciation, which gives you a larger deduction the first few years you own the asset and smaller deductions in later years.

You can easily calculate your annual depreciation deductions for personal property you use in your rental activity by using accounting and tax preparation software, online calculators, or by using the charts in IRS Publication 946, *How to Depreciate Property.*

Personal Property Converted to Rental Use

When you begin to rent out your main home or vacation home you've used personally, you'll be converting personal property to rental use. You may take a depreciation deduction for property you already own and have used personally and then convert for use in for your rental activity but it does not qualify for bonus depreciation, the de minimis safe harbor, or Section 179 expensing. You must deduct the cost using regular depreciation. The amount you depreciate is the lesser of:

- its fair market value on the date you convert it for use in your rental activity, or
- its cost, prorated, if needed, by the percentage rental activity use.

Personal property like furniture and appliances usually goes down substantially in value soon after it's put to use, so the fair market value will usually be lower.

> **EXAMPLE:** Jean owns a three-bedroom home with a large basement family room. She decides to convert the family room into a full-time short-term room rental. She moves into the room a bed, dresser, chair, and desk that she and her family had been using in other rooms in the house. When she lists the family room for rent, she is converting this furniture from personal to rental use. She may depreciate the lesser of its fair market value or its cost when she first lists the room for rent. Used furniture ordinarily goes down in value over time. Jean paid $3,000 for the furniture when new, but she determines by looking at eBay and similar listings that it is worth only $500 when she lists the room for rent. Thus, she may only depreciate $500. She does this over five years using regular depreciation as described above.

If you wish, you may separately depreciate all the personal property in your home, vacation home, or other home that you convert to rental use. For example, you can take a deduction for the fair market value of the stove, refrigerator, dishwasher, furniture, carpets, and drapes. However, the value of these items is usually low, so it's often not worth the time and trouble involved, especially since you'll have to reduce your deduction by the amount of time you use your home personally. For example, if you have a used refrigerator in your home with a fair market value of $100 when you converted the property to rental use, and you rent the home 30% of the time, you'll be able to depreciate $30 over five years. If you're interested in doing this, you'll find a detailed discussion in Chapter 6 of *Every Landlord's Tax Deduction Guide,* by Stephen Fishman (Nolo). ●

The Pass-Through Tax Deduction

The Tax Cuts and Jobs Act established a brand new income tax deduction for owners of pass-through businesses, which includes most short-term rental hosts. This is commonly referred to as the pass-through deduction or qualified business income (QBI) deduction. If you qualify, you may be able to deduct from your income taxes up to 20% of your net income from your short-term rental business, reducing your effective income tax rate on such income by 20%. This deduction began in 2018 and is scheduled to last through 2025. Following are the basic requirements short-term hosts must satisfy to qualify for this complex deduction. This deduction is available for all types of pass-through businesses, but this chapter focuses how it works for short-term rental hosts.

Your Rental Activity Must Be a Business

To qualify for the pass-through deduction, your short-term rental activity must qualify as a business for tax purposes, not an investment activity or not-for-profit activity. This is determined under the general rules used to determine whether any activity is a business. (I.R.C. § 162; IRS Reg. 1.199A-1(b)(14).) These rules are discussed in detail in Chapter 4.

As discussed in Chapter 4, most short-term rental activities should qualify as a business, particularly if they earn profits most years. However, hosts who rent their property at below market rates or make no effort to rent it at all are likely to run afoul of this requirement.

The rules for determining whether an activity qualifies as a business are somewhat vague and ambiguous. To provide landlords with absolute certainty, the IRS created an optional safe harbor rule. Under this rule, landlords are automatically deemed to be in business solely for purposes of the pass-through deduction if they:

- perform a total of 250 hours of real estate rental services each year (including work performed by employees and agents)
- keep records documenting the real estate services performed, and

- keep separate books and records showing income and expenses for each rental real estate enterprise. (IRS Notice 2019-7.)

However, you can't use this safe harbor rule if the property involved is used as a residence for tax purposes (as defined in I.R.C. § 280A, which is covered in Chapter 3). This means you can't use the safe harbor if you or family members live in the property more than 14 days during the year; or if you use it more than 10% of the number of days during the year the property is rented for a fair rental. This eliminates most short-term rental hosts.

If you do live in a property less than 14 days, you can take advantage of the safe harbor rule. But, you likely don't need it. And, remember, its use is purely optional. For detailed guidance on the rental property pass-through business safe harbor rule, see *Every Landlord's Tax Guide*, by Stephen Fishman (Nolo).

Your Rental Activity Must Be a Pass-Through Business

You have to have a pass-through business to qualify for this deduction. A pass-through business is one in which the profits (or losses) are passed through the business and the owners pay tax on the money on their individual tax returns at their individual tax rates. Luckily, virtually all short-term hosts operate as pass-through businesses. Most short-term hosts own their property individually, as a joint tenancy with their spouse, or with one or more individuals as tenants in common. All these ownership forms qualify as pass-through businesses.

A minority of short-term hosts own the property they rent through a business entity, usually a limited liability company (LLC) or partnership. These also qualify as pass-through businesses. S corporations also qualify, but are rarely used for rental property. Regular C corporations don't qualify for the pass-through deduction; but, for a variety of tax reasons, C corporations are almost never used for rental property.

You Must Have Qualified Business Income

Hosts may qualify to deduct from their income tax up to 20% of their "qualified business income" (QBI). QBI is the net income (profit) your short-term rental business earns during the year. You determine this by subtracting all your regular short-term rental deductions from your total short-term rental income. Your net rental income or loss is listed in the "Total rental real estate and royalty income (or loss)" line at the bottom of Schedule E.

QBI does not include:

- short-term or long-term capital gain or loss—for example, the capital gain (or loss) earned from selling your property
- dividend income or interest income
- guaranteed payments to partners in partnerships or LLC members, or
- business income earned outside of the United States— such as property outside the United States you rent to short-term guests.

You can benefit from the pass-through deduction only if your short-term rental business earns a profit for the year. You get no deduction if your rental business shows a net loss because your QBI will be zero.

> **EXAMPLE:** Ann rents her home to short-term guests. This year her guests paid her $12,000 in rent and she incurred $6,000 in total deductible expenses, including depreciation. Her QBI is $6,000.

> **EXAMPLE:** Bill owns a main home and a vacation home that he rents to short-term guests. This year, the short-term rental of his main home earned a profit of $10,000, while the rental of the vacation home incurred a loss of $4,000. His QBI for his short-term rental business is $6,000.

If you have other nonrental businesses, QBI is determined separately for each separate business you own. If one or more of your businesses lose money, you deduct the loss from the QBI from your profitable businesses. If you have a "qualified business loss"—that is, your net QBI is zero or less—you get no pass-through deduction for the year. Any loss is carried forward to the next year and the pass-through deduction for that year (or the next future year with positive QBI) is reduced (but not below zero) by 20% of the loss.

> **EXAMPLE:** During 2020, George earned $20,000 in QBI from his short- term rental business and had a $50,000 loss from his Bitcoin mining business. He had a $30,000 qualified business loss, so he gets no pass-through deduction for 2020 and his loss must be carried forward to 2021. His pass-through deduction for 2021 must be reduced by 20% of his $30,000 loss, or $6,000.

You Must Have Taxable Income

To determine your pass-through deduction, you must first figure your total taxable income for the year (not counting the pass-through deduction). This is your total taxable income from all sources (short-term rental and other business, investment, and job income) minus deductions, including the standard deduction ($12,400 for singles and $24,800 for marrieds filing jointly in 2020) or your itemized deductions. However, you do not include net capital gains for the year in your taxable income (such amounts already receive preferential tax treatment). If you're married and file jointly, include your spouse's income in your taxable income.

Your pass-through deduction can never exceed 20% of your taxable income. This limitation won't adversely impact most hosts because they typically have income in addition to that earned through the short-term rental activity.

> **EXAMPLE:** Larry earned $10,000 in profit from his short-term rental business this year. He had $90,000 in job income and took the standard deduction. His taxable income is $87,600 ($100,000 − $12,400 standard deduction = $87,600). His pass-through deduction cannot exceed 20% x $87,600 = $17,520. His pass-through deduction is $2,000 (20% x $10,000), so the limit has no practical effect.

Calculating Your Pass-Through Deduction

How you calculate the pass-through deduction depends on your annual taxable income. The rules differ for 2020 taxable income:
- up to $163,300 ($326,600 if married)
- between $163,301 to $213,300 ($326,601–$426,600 if married), and
- above $213,300 ($426,600 if married).

Taxable Income Up to $163,300 ($326,600 if Married)

If your 2020 taxable income is at or below $163,300 if single, or $326,600 if married filing jointly, your pass-through deduction is equal to 20% of your qualified business income (QBI). However, as discussed above, the deduction may not exceed 20% of your taxable income.

> **EXAMPLE:** Tom is single and earned $10,400 in QBI during 2020 from his short-term rental business. He also earned $102,000 in job income and took the $12,400 standard deduction. His total taxable income for the year is $100,000 (($10,400 + $102,000) − $12,400 = $100,000). His pass-through deduction is 20% x $10,400 = $2,080. He may deduct $2,080 from his income taxes.

If your taxable income is at or below the $163,300/$326,600 thresholds, that's all there is to the pass-through deduction. You're effectively taxed on only 80% of your short-term rental business income.

Taxable Income Above $213,300 ($426,600 if Married)

If your 2020 taxable income is above $213,300 (single) or $426,600 (married filing jointly), your maximum possible pass-through deduction is 20% of your QBI, just like at the lower income levels. However, when your income is this high, a W-2 wage/business property limitation takes effect. Your deduction is limited to the greater of:

- 50% of your pro rata share of W-2 employee wages paid by your rental business, or
- 25% of W-2 wages PLUS 2.5% of the acquisition cost of the depreciable property used in your short-term rental business.

Few short-term rental hosts have employees. They manage their short-term rental businesses themselves or hire property management companies who are not W-2 employees. Thus, they have zero wages upon which to base their pass-through deduction. Fortunately, the pass-through deduction may alternatively be based on 2.5% of the acquisition cost of your depreciable property plus 25% of W-2 wages (which will likely be zero).

The business property must be depreciable long-term property used in the production of income. This would include your home or other real property you rent to short-term guests, and any other depreciable long-term property you use in your short-term rental business, such as gardening equipment. The cost is its unadjusted basis—the original acquisition cost, minus the cost of land. If you added improvements after you purchased the property, you should add their acquisition cost to the unadjusted basis of the property. You must reduce your acquisition cost by the percentage of the year you personally use the property. To do this, multiply the total acquisition cost by your rental use percentage. (See Chapter 10.)

> **EXAMPLE:** Lisa purchased her home for $250,000 and allocates
> $50,000 of the cost to the land, resulting in a $200,000 acquisition
> cost. She rents the home 20% of the year to short-term guests and
> personally uses it 80% of the year. Her unadjusted acquisition basis is
> 20% x $200,000= $40,000.

In the case of personal property like equipment or computers, it
makes no difference whether you deducted the full cost in the first year
with bonus depreciation or Section 179. However, you can't count any
personal property you deducted with the de minimis safe harbor, safe
harbor for small taxpayers, or routine maintenance safe harbors. Such
property is not considered depreciable property for tax purposes.

You can include any property you acquire during the year and still
own at the end of the year. You can't include any property you sell any
time during the year.

The 2.5% deduction can be taken during the entire depreciation
period for the property. For your real property, this is 27.5 years if you
classify the property as residential property or 39 years if it is classified as
nonresidential property (see Chapter 7). Personal property has a shorter
depreciation period—five or seven years. However, for purposes of the
pass-through deduction, the depreciation period can be no shorter than
ten years. Thus, the cost of personal property can be included in your
2.5% deduction a full ten years after purchase.

> **EXAMPLE:** Aaron, a single taxpayer, purchased a three-bedroom
> home in San Francisco 20 years ago that he rents out to short-term
> guests 25% of the year. This year, he earned a profit of $15,000 from his
> short-term rental business. He has no employees. His taxable income
> is $250,000, so the W-2/property limitation applies in full to his pass-
> through deduction. Since he has no employees, his deduction is limited
> to 2.5% of the acquisition basis of his home. He paid $300,000 for the
> home and allocates $60,000 of the cost to the land. The acquisition

> basis in the home is $240,000 x 25% = $60,000. Thus, his pass-through deduction is limited to $1,500 (2.5 % x $60,000 = $1,500). Had the W-2/property limit not applied, Aaron's pass-through deduction would have been 20% x $15,000 = $3,000. Thus, he lost half his deduction.

Property that is fully depreciated can't be included in the 2.5% property calculation. Thus, hosts at these income levels who purchased their home, vacation home, or other property they rent to short-term guests many years ago and have fully depreciated all or most of it, may end up with little or no pass-through deduction.

Taxable Income $163,301 to $213,300 ($326,601 to $426,600 if Married)

If your 2020 taxable income is $163,301 to $213,300 (single) or $326,601 to $426,600 (married filing jointly), the W-2 wages/property limitation described above is phased in—that is, only part of your deduction is subject to the limit and the rest is based on 20% of your QBI. The phase-in range is $50,000 for singles and $100,000 for marrieds. For example, the limit would be 50% phased in for married taxpayers with taxable income of $376,600 ($50,000 over $326,600), which equals 50% of the $100,000 phase-in range. At the top of the income range ($213,300 for singles, $426,600 for marrieds), your entire deduction is subject to the W-2 wages/business property limit.

Pass-Through Deduction Thresholds, Limits, and Phase-Ins (2020)

Taxable Income:	Taxable Income:	Taxable Income:
Single: Up to $163,300 Married: Up to $326,600	Single: $163,301–$213,300 Married: $326,601–$426,600	Single: $213,301 or more Married: $426,601 or more
Full 20% deduction No W-2/property limit	20% deduction subject to phase-in of W-2/property limit	20% deduction permitted but fully subject to W-2/property limit

Taking the Pass-Through Deduction

The pass-through deduction is a personal deduction you may take on your Form 1040 whether or not you itemize. You don't take it on Schedule E. To compute and claim the deduction, you must complete IRS Form 8995, *Qualified Business Income Deduction Simplified Computation*. But if your taxable income exceeds the applicable threshold amount, you should file Form 8995-A, *Qualified Business Income Deduction*. You then transfer the amount of the deduction to a line on your Form 1040.

The pass-through deduction is not an "above the line" deduction on the first page of Form 1040 that reduces your adjusted gross income (AGI). Thus, for example, it does not reduce your income for purposes of qualifying for health insurance credits under the Affordable Care Act. Moreover, the deduction only reduces income taxes, not Social Security or Medicare taxes (hosts who do not provide substantial services to their guests need not pay Social Security or Medicare taxes on their short-term rental income; see Chapter 2).

Strategies to Maximize the Pass-Through Deduction

There are several ways landlords can increase their pass-through deduction.

Increase Rental Income

First, your pass-through deduction is always limited to 20% of your net short-term rental income (QBI). Thus, the more rental income you have, the greater your deduction will be. You can increase your short-term net rental income by renting your property more of the time to short-term guests, increasing your rental rates, or both.

Buy New Property to Rent Short-Term

Second, as shown above, the maximum pass-through deduction is 20% of your net rental income (your QBI). But if your 2020 taxable income exceeds $213,300 if you're single, or $426,600 if you're married filing jointly, your deduction will be limited to the greater of (1) 50% of W-2 wages you pay to employees, or (2) 25% of W-2 wages plus 2.5% of the unadjusted basis (acquisition cost) of your rental property. In between these two thresholds the W-2/property limit is phased in. Few hosts have employees, so the limit will usually be based on 2.5% of your unadjusted basis in your property. If this amount is equal to or more than 20% of QBI, there's no problem—your deduction will still be equal to 20% of your QBI. But, if it's less, you'll lose part of your deduction. If, for example, you have $100,000 unadjusted basis in your property, your deduction will be limited to $2,500 (2.5% x 100,000 = $2,500). If you earned $20,000 in profit from your short-term rental business, you'd lose $1,500 you could have deducted had the W-2/property limit not applied—your deduction would have been 20% x $20,000 = $4,000. If you're in this situation, you can increase your deduction by buying new property to rent short term, which will increase your total unadjusted basis to be multiplied by 2.5%.

Keep Your Taxable Income Below W-2/Property Thresholds

If the W-2/property limitation reduces or eliminates your deduction, you could seek to keep your taxable income for the year below the full W-2/property phase-in amount: $213,300 for singles, or $426,600 for marrieds filing jointly (2020). If you keep your taxable income at or below $163,300 (single) or $326,600 (married), you'll completely avoid the phase-in of the W-2/property limitation and qualify for the full 20% of QBI deduction. Your taxable income is your total income (not including capital gains) minus your deductions. If you don't itemize, this would include your standard deduction ($12,400 for singles, $24,800 for marrieds in 2020). Thus, if you take the standard deduction, you could have $175,700 in income (single) or $351,400 (married) and come within the income limits to qualify for the 20% of QBI deduction.

If your income is at or near these limits, there are lots of things you can do to reduce your taxable income for the year. For example, you can contribute to retirement accounts such as IRAs and 401(k)s— your contributions are deducted from your taxable income subject to annual limits (in 2020, business owners can contribute up to $57,000 to retirement plans). You could also give money to charity if you're so inclined (make sure you're able to itemize your personal deductions).

Prorating Your Deductions

M ost short-term rental hosts don't rent out their property 100% of the time. Instead, they live in the property part of the time and rent all or part of it part of the time. If you fall into this category, it's important to remember that you don't get to deduct expenses for your personal use or any other nonrental use of the property. Instead, you must prorate your expenses between your rental and nonrental use. You do this by calculating the percentage of time the property is rented and, in the case of room rentals, the percentage of the property rented. Then you prorate your total expenses by your rental percentage.

Direct Expenses Are Fully Deductible

Not all the expenses you incur in your short-term rental activity need to be prorated. You can fully deduct the money you spend specifically to rent your home and run your short-term rental activity. Such direct expenses do not have a personal element. They would not have been incurred if you were not engaged in your rental activity. These direct expenses include:

- fees or other charges by rental platforms
- local or state licensing or registration fees
- advertising your rental
- credit checks for your guests
- any expenses you incur to photograph your property or create a good listing for Airbnb or any other rental platform
- the cost of purchasing a lockbox or having duplicate keys made
- the cost of storing your belongings while guests are staying in your home
- legal and professional fees for the rental activity (see Chapter 5)
- office expenses for your rental activity (see Chapter 5)
- mileage and travel expenses for your rental activity (see Chapter 5)
- additional insurance coverage you purchase for your rental activity (see Chapter 5), and

- fees charged by a management company you hire to handle your rental (see Chapter 5).

You can also fully deduct all expenses that are solely for the benefit of your guests. These include amenities you provide your guests and don't use yourself, such as bedding, linens, toiletries, food, books, and games. It would also include the cost of a second phone line, computer, or television that you provide for your guests' exclusive use.

Expenses That Must Be Prorated

All your expenses other than direct expenses are only partially deductible —they must be prorated between your rental and nonrental use of the property. These are expenses that apply to the entire home or other property you rent and also use personally. If you own the home or other property, these expenses include:

- depreciation of the rental building and personal property in the building (see Chapter 7)
- mortgage interest and private mortgage insurance (see Chapter 5)
- real property taxes (see Chapter 5), and
- casualty and theft losses (see Chapter 5).

If you rent the home or other property, you may deduct a prorated amount of your rent. You can also deduct personal property you purchase and use for the rental activity, such as furnishings.

Whether you're an owner or renter, you may deduct your prorated operating expenses for the entire home, including:

- repairs (see Chapter 5)
- maintenance, cleaning, trash removal, condo/HOA fees, utilities, Internet, and cable TV (see Chapter 5), and
- regular homeowners' or renters' insurance (see Chapter 5).

You can only deduct as a rental expense, the expenses allocated to your rental use. How you do this allocation depends on whether you rent your entire home or a room or rooms (or part of a room) during the year.

Renting Your Entire Home

If you rent your entire home to short-term guests, you allocate your prorated expenses according to the percentage of time the property was rented out to guests during the year. You must first determine how many rental, personal, and not-in-use days you have for the year. How to do this is explained below (see "Calculating Personal and Rental Days"). You then divide the number of rental days by the total number of days the property was used (personal use days + rental days). You can use the following simple formula: Days rented % = (rental use days) ÷ (rental use days + personal use days). Expenses allocated to the days rented period may be deducted the same as any other rental expense.

EXAMPLE: Miranda's vacation home was used a total of 180 days during the year: Miranda used it personally for 90 days and she rented it to various short-term guests through Airbnb for 90 days. It remained vacant (not used by Miranda or offered for rent) for 180 days. She reports her rental income and expenses on IRS Schedule E. The rental days percentage is 50%, calculated as follows: 90 ÷ (90 + 90) = 50%. This percentage must be used to allocate Miranda's expenses that are not fully deductible. Miranda may deduct the following amounts on her Schedule E:

Expense	Amount	Deduction Percentage	Deduction Amount
Direct expenses (Airbnb fees, licensing fees, mileage)	$1,000	100%	$1,000
Real estate taxes	$3,000	50%	$1,500
Mortgage interest	$12,000	50%	$6,000
Operating expenses (utilities, repairs, insurance)	$2,000	50%	$1,000
Depreciation	$5,000	50%	$2,500
Total	$23,000		$12,000

Miranda earned $15,000 from her rentals, so she earned a $3,000 profit that she must report on Schedule E. In addition, Miranda can deduct 50% of her mortgage interest and real estate taxes as a personal itemized deduction on her Schedule A.

Renting a Room in Your Home

If you rent a room or rooms in your home (or part of a room), instead of the entire home, you must allocate your partial deductions not only by the amount of time the room or rooms were rented out to guests, but by the amount of space in your home that was rented out as well. First, calculate your rental use days percentage as described above, then multiply this by the percentage of the home that was rented. Here's the formula: Rental use % = (days rented %) x (area rented %). You can only deduct the rental use percentage of your prorated expenses. Thus, for example, if Miranda in the previous example only rented out a room in her home that amounted to 20% of the entire home, her rental use percentage would be 50% x 20% = 10%. She would only be able to deduct 10% of her prorated expenses.

You can determine your area rented percentage by multiplying the square footage rented by the overall square footage of your home. Here's the formula: Area rented % = (square footage rented) ÷ (overall square footage). Alternatively, if the rooms in your home are about the same size (not counting bathrooms, garages, attics, or similar rooms), you can use the number of rooms rented divided by the total number of rooms to calculate your area rented percentage.

> EXAMPLE: Jack owns a two-bedroom condo in Honolulu. He rents one bedroom to travelers through Airbnb, taking up 20% of the space in his unit, for 100 days during the year and lives in the unit throughout the year. His rental use of the bedroom is 100 days and his personal use is 265 days. To allocate his expenses between rental and personal use, his rental days are treated as being 100, and personal days are 265. Thus his days rented percentage is 100 ÷ (100 + 265) = 27%. His rental

use percentage is 5% (27% days rented x 20% area rented = 5%). Thus, he can deduct 5% of his prorated expenses and 100% of his direct expenses. He deducts his expenses as follows:

Expense	Amount	Amount Allocated to Rental Use	Amount Deducted
Mortgage interest	$30,000	$1,500 (5%) rental use)	$1,500
Property tax	$6,000	$300 (5% rental use)	$300
Direct expenses	$9,000	$9,000 (100% rental use)	$9,000
Operating expenses	$12,000	$600 (5% rental use)	$600
Depreciation	$15,000	$750 (5% rental use)	$750
Total	$72,000	$12,150	$12,150

Jack deducts his rental income and expenses on Schedule E. Jack may also deduct 95% of his property tax and mortgage interest as a personal itemized deduction on his Schedule A. This is the amount of taxes and rent allocated to the time he personally used the condo.

Calculating Personal and Rental Days

To allocate your expenses, you must determine how many days during the year your property is used personally by you, how many days it's rented out to others, and how many days it's not in use. You must also provide this information when you complete IRS Schedule E for your rental. As you might expect, there are tax rules for determining this.

> **TIP**
> **Keep careful track of all guest stays at your home, including those by relatives.** A good way to prove to the IRS how long your guests—paying and otherwise—stayed in your vacation home is to have them all sign and date a visitors' book. You can create one yourself or buy one from a stationery store.

Calculating Personal Use

A day of personal use is any day, or part of a day, that your home or apartment is used by:

- you or any co-owner of the property
- a member of your family or a member of the family of any co-owner (unless the family member uses the home as his or her main home and pays a fair rental price)
- anyone under an arrangement that lets you use some of the home, or
- anyone at less than a fair rental price. (I.R.C. § 280A(d)(2).)

For these purposes, family members include your brothers and sisters, half-brothers and half-sisters, spouse, ancestors (parents, grandparents, and so on), and lineal descendants (children, grandchildren, and so on). However, renting your home to your aunts, uncles, nieces, nephews, cousins, or friends does not count as personal use. If you rent your home to anyone in this group of people for a fair market price, it is considered rental use.

What Is a Fair Rental Price?

A fair rental price is the amount of rent that a person not related to you would be willing to pay. A rental price is not fair if it is substantially less than rents charged for similar properties. To determine if the price you charge is fair, look at rental listings for similar properties on Airbnb and other short-term rental platforms. You should ask the following questions when comparing properties to yours to determine if they are similar:

- Are they used for the same purpose?
- Are they approximately the same size?
- Are they in approximately the same condition?
- Do they have similar furnishings?
- Are they in similar locations?

The IRS says that, if the answer to any one of these questions is no, the properties probably are not similar. You can also ask for a written opinion from a real estate professional familiar with the short-term home rental market in the area that your rental price is fair. Be sure to keep records of how you determined the fair rental price.

Days Used for Repairs and Maintenance

Any day that you spend working substantially full time (at least eight hours) repairing and maintaining your property is not counted as a day of personal use. These days are not rental days either; instead, the property is treated as not being used at all on those days. You don't have to count the day as a day of personal use even if family members use the property for recreation on the same day. It's a good idea to maintain and keep documentation showing that you performed repairs or maintenance on your rental, rather than using it for personal use. This can include receipts, time logs, and work reports.

> EXAMPLE: You own a cabin in the mountains that you rent out during the summer. You spend three days at the cabin each May, working full time to repair anything that was damaged over the winter and to get the cabin ready for the summer. You also spend three days each September working full time to repair any damage done by renters and getting the cabin ready for the winter. These six days do not count as days of personal (or rental) use even if your family uses the cabin while you are repairing it.

You also don't need to count days you spend seeking tenants or dealing with realtors as personal days.

Calculating Rental Use

Any day you rent your home at a fair market rent is a day of rental use no matter whom you rent it to, unless it's a family member who doesn't live there full time. Any day you rent your home to anyone for less than a fair rental price is considered a day of personal use. Days you offer your home for rent, but are unable to actually rent it to a guest, don't count as rental days. Days the home is vacant don't count as rental or personal use days.

Personal Use Days	Rental Use Days	Not-in-Use Days
Days you use the property	Days property rented for fair market rent	Days the property is vacant
Days property rented for less than fair market rent		Days property offered for rent, but not rented
Days family members use the property (unless they live there full time and pay market rate rent)		Days used for maintenance and repairs

Putting Your Calculations Together

Let's look at a comprehensive example to see how these rules operate. Carlos owns a home that he used himself for 309 days during the year. While he was out of town on business various times during the year, he rented the entire home as follows:

- four days to his mother, who paid nothing
- 30 days through Airbnb to guests (tourists) who paid a fair market rental
- 20 days when Carlos was out of town the property was vacant because he couldn't find any guests to stay there, and
- two days to a friend from the office who paid a below-fair-market price.

Carlos's own use is personal use. The four days his mother used the house for free are also personal days. The 30 days he rented it to strangers for a fair market price are rental days. The two days he let a friend use it for a below-market rental are personal days. His totals for the year are:

Rental days = 30

Personal days = 315

Not-in-use days = 20

(Carlos's rental use percentage is 9% (30 ÷ 345 = .086).

Using the *Bolton* Method to Allocate Mortgage Interest and Property Tax

You have another option for allocating the rental use percentage of your mortgage interest and property tax—often referred to as the *Bolton* method, based on the court case that established it. Instead of basing your allocation on the total number of days the property is actually used and not counting not-in-use days, you count all 365 days to figure your rental use percentage for mortgage interest and property tax. This gives you smaller rental expense for these costs. However, you may be able to deduct the amount allocated to personal use as a personal itemized deduction. If so, this can be to your advantage if you have a rental loss for the year and are subject to the vacation home rules, which severely restrict your ability to deduct rental losses. See Chapter 3 for a detailed discussion.

Reporting Rental Income on Your Tax Return

When you engage in a short-term rental activity, you'll have to file an additional schedule with your tax return to report your rental income and expenses to the IRS. Most short-term rental hosts must file IRS Schedule E. This chapter shows how to fill out this tax form.

Most Hosts Use Schedule E to Report Rental Income

Most short-term rental hosts must file IRS Schedule E, *Supplemental Income and Loss,* with their annual tax return to report their rental income and expenses. You list all your rental income and expenses on this form. You then subtract the expenses from the income to determine if you have net rental income or a rental loss for the year. Any net rental income is added to your other income on your Form 1040. A rental loss may or may not be deductible.

If you own your rental activity as a single individual, you will file Schedule E to report your rental income and expenses, subject to the exceptions noted below. You also use Schedule E if you form a single-member limited liability company (LLC) to operate your rental activity. This is because a single-member LLC is a "disregarded entity" for tax purposes—it's as if it doesn't exist. Schedule E is also usually filed for short-term rentals owned and operated by two or more people. If you own the property with your spouse and you file a joint tax return, you and your spouse can report your rental income and expenses on a single Schedule E that you file with your joint Form 1040 tax return.

If you own the property with one or more people you aren't married to and don't form an entity like an LLC, then each owner may file a Schedule E to report his or her share of the expenses and income from the rental activity. Co-owners who are tenants in common or joint tenants do not become partners in a partnership with each other as long as all they do is own rental property together and merely maintain, repair, and rent it. That is, they don't provide their guests with substantial services as explained below (see "Hosts Who Don't File Schedule E"). (IRS Reg. § 1.761-1(a), IRS Reg. § 301.7701(a)(2).) Such co-owners don't need to file a separate partnership tax return, which can be complex and expensive.

However, there are certain situations where hosts don't use Schedule E. These are where:

- Multiple owners form a business entity—typically an LLC— to operate the rental activity.
- Hosts provide their guests with substantial services.
- Married hosts elect qualified joint venture status.
- Married hosts live in a community property state and elect to treat their rental activity as a sole proprietorship.
- The rental activity is a not-for-profit activity.

If you fall into one of these categories, you file a different form to report your rental income and expenses. See "Hosts Who Don't File Schedule E," below for more information.

Schedule E Line-by-Line

Completing Schedule E is a relatively straightforward process. You fill out only the first page, which is called Part I. (Part I is also used for royalties, which have nothing to do with rental property.) Parts II–V on the second page are only used by partnerships, S corporations, estates, trusts, and real estate mortgage investment conduits (REMICs, a type of real estate investment).

You separately list on the schedule your income and expenses for each property you rent, whether full or part time. Schedule E is designed to be used for up to three rental properties, labeled A, B, and C; there are separate columns for each property. If you have more than three rental properties, complete and attach as many Schedule Es as you need for them all. But fill in Lines 23a through 26 on only one Schedule E. The figures there should be the combined totals for all properties reported.

Schedule E (Form 1040)—page 1

SCHEDULE E (Form 1040 or 1040-SR) Department of the Treasury Internal Revenue Service (99)	**Supplemental Income and Loss** (From rental real estate, royalties, partnerships, S corporations, estates, trusts, REMICs, etc.) ▶ Attach to Form 1040, 1040-SR, 1040-NR, or 1041. ▶ Go to *www.irs.gov/ScheduleE* for instructions and the latest information.	OMB No. 1545-0074 **2019** Attachment Sequence No. **13**

Name(s) shown on return   Your social security number

Part I   **Income or Loss From Rental Real Estate and Royalties**   Note: If you are in the business of renting personal property, use **Schedule C** (see instructions). If you are an individual, report farm rental income or loss from **Form 4835** on page 2, line 40.

A Did you make any payments in 2019 that would require you to file Form(s) 1099? (see instructions) . . . . . ☐ **Yes** ☐ **No**

B If "Yes," did you or will you file required Forms 1099? . . . . ☐ **Yes** ☐ **No**

1a Physical address of each property (street, city, state, ZIP code)

A

B

C

1b	Type of Property (from list below)	2	For each rental real estate property listed above, report the number of fair rental and personal use days. Check the **QJV** box only if you meet the requirements to file as a qualified joint venture. See instructions.		Fair Rental Days	Personal Use Days	QJV
A				A			☐
B				B			☐
C				C			☐

Type of Property:

1 Single Family Residence   3 Vacation/Short-Term Rental   5 Land   7 Self-Rental

2 Multi-Family Residence   4 Commercial   6 Royalties   8 Other (describe)

Income:	Properties:		A	B	C
3 Rents received		3			
4 Royalties received		4			
Expenses:					
5 Advertising		5			
6 Auto and travel (see instructions)		6			
7 Cleaning and maintenance		7			
8 Commissions.		8			
9 Insurance		9			
10 Legal and other professional fees		10			
11 Management fees		11			
12 Mortgage interest paid to banks, etc. (see instructions)		12			
13 Other interest.		13			
14 Repairs.		14			
15 Supplies		15			
16 Taxes		16			
17 Utilities		17			
18 Depreciation expense or depletion		18			
19 Other (list) ▶		19			
20 Total expenses. Add lines 5 through 19		20			
21 Subtract line 20 from line 3 (rents) and/or 4 (royalties). If result is a (loss), see instructions to find out if you must file **Form 6198**		21			
22 Deductible rental real estate loss after limitation, if any, on **Form 8582** (see instructions)		22	( )(	)(	)

23a	Total of all amounts reported on line 3 for all rental properties	23a	
b	Total of all amounts reported on line 4 for all royalty properties	23b	
c	Total of all amounts reported on line 12 for all properties	23c	
d	Total of all amounts reported on line 18 for all properties	23d	
e	Total of all amounts reported on line 20 for all properties	23e	

24	**Income.** Add positive amounts shown on line 21. **Do not** include any losses	24	
25	**Losses.** Add royalty losses from line 21 and rental real estate losses from line 22. Enter total losses here .	25	( )
26	**Total rental real estate and royalty income or (loss).** Combine lines 24 and 25. Enter the result here. If Parts II, III, IV, and line 40 on page 2 do not apply to you, also enter this amount on Schedule 1 (Form 1040 or 1040-SR), line 5, or Form 1040-NR, line 18. Otherwise, include this amount in the total on line 41 on page 2	26	

For Paperwork Reduction Act Notice, see the separate instructions.   Cat. No. 11344L   Schedule E (Form 1040 or 1040-SR) 2019

If you own only a part interest in a rental property, report only your share of the property's income and expenses.

> **EXAMPLE:** Betty and Bettina each own a 50% interest in a vacation home they rent out to short-term guests. Betty reports 50% of the property's income and expenses on her Schedule E, and Bettina reports the other 50% on her Schedule E.

Lines A and B: Filing IRS Forms 1099

Line A asks whether you made any payments during the year that required you to file IRS Forms 1099. If you answer yes, you have to answer in Line B whether you have already filed, "or will you file," the forms. Obviously, you should answer "yes" on Line B if you answered "yes" on Line A. If you haven't filed the required 1099 forms, you should do so as soon as possible.

1099 forms are information returns used to report various types of payments to the IRS. There are several types of 1099 forms. The one that usually has to be filed by rental property owners is Form 1099-NEC. You must file Form 1099-NEC if (1) your rental activity constitutes a business for tax purposes, and (2) you hire an independent contractor to perform services for your activity and pay him or her by cash or check more than $600 during the year—for example, you hire a repairperson or gardener. You don't need to report payments by credit card or PayPal or any other similar electronic payment services. See Chapter 11 for a detailed discussion of filing Form 1099-NEC.

These questions are an attempt by the IRS to encourage landlords and others who file Schedule E to file all required 1099s. This is part of the IRS's ongoing effort to prevent businesses from failing to report all their income.

Line 1a-1b: Physical address and type of property

In Line 1, list your property's street address, city or town, state, and ZIP code. In the next box, provide the applicable number code showing the type of property.

Line 2: Dual-use properties

This portion of Schedule E is extremely important for short-term rental hosts. You list here the actual number of days the property was occupied by renters (fair rental days), and the number of days it was used by you or your family for personal purposes (personal use days). Personal use includes not only use by you or your relatives, but anyone you let use the property without paying fair market rent. (See Chapter 9 for detailed guidance on how to calculate your personal and rental days.)

You must prorate your expenses based on the number of days the property was used as a rental versus the days it was used as a personal residence. (See Chapter 9 for detailed guidance on how to prorate your deductions.) If you incurred a loss and personally used the property more than 14 days or more than 10% of the rental days, you'll be subject to the vacation home tax rules. These prevent you from deducting your losses, and require you to take your deductions in a prescribed order on Schedule E. (See Chapter 3 for detailed guidance.)

If you didn't use the rental property for personal purposes, enter zero in the "Personal Use Days" column and 365 in the "Fair Rental Days" column (assuming you rented the property the entire year).

Line 3: Rents received

Enter your total annual rental income in Line 3. This will primarily consist of the rent your guests pay you. But it could also include:
- garage or other parking charges
- security deposits you retain to pay for repairs or other expenses
- the value of services tenants provide in lieu of rent, or
- payments guests make to you for repairs or other expenses.

A security deposit you receive from a guest is not rental income unless you keep all or part of it when the guest leaves.

Line 4: Royalties received

Leave this blank unless you have royalty income—for example, income from copyrights or patents you inherited or purchased, or mineral leases. If you are a self-employed writer, inventor, artist, and so on, you report your royalty income and expenses on Schedule C, *Profit or Loss From Business (Sole Proprietorship)*.

Expenses (Lines 5–20)

You list your expenses in Lines 5–20. When you rent your property part time, many of your expenses must be prorated based on how much of the time you rent the property—and, if you only rent a room or rooms, how much of the property you rent. (See Chapter 9.) You only list the prorated amounts in Schedule E.

Your expenses must be broken down into the following expense categories.

Line 5: Advertising

This includes website expenses, photography costs, classified ads, and other advertising expenses to rent your property.

Line 6: Auto and travel

This category includes both local and long-distance travel expenses. (See Chapter 5.) If you have both types of expenses, you must add them together. If you leased or rented the vehicle, show the lease payments on Line 19. If you use the actual expense method to deduct your vehicle expenses, show your depreciation expense in Line 18, but list all your other expenses in Line 6.

Line 7: Cleaning and maintenance

This includes janitorial services, gardening, cleaning carpets, drapes, and rugs. Do not include repairs here—repairs are done to fix property after it's broken; maintenance keeps your property in good working order so it won't break down.

Line 8: Commissions

These consist primarily of the fees you pay to online rental platforms like Airbnb to list your property for short-term rental.

Line 9: Insurance

You may fully deduct any insurance coverage you purchase just for your short-term rental activity, such as additional liability coverage for short-term guests. The cost of other insurance coverage for your home, such as homeowners' or renters' insurance, must be prorated based on the percentage of rental use of the property (see Chapter 9). However, you may only deduct insurance coverage for one year at a time. If you pay for more than one year of coverage, only deduct the amount that was for coverage for the current tax year.

Line 10: Legal and other professional fees

This includes tax advice and preparing tax forms for your rental activity. (See Chapter 5.)

Line 11: Management fees

These are fees charged by property management companies. If you hire a manager to handle your short-term rental activity, deduct the total cost here.

Line 12: Mortgage interest paid to banks

If you have a mortgage on your property, you may deduct a prorated amount on Schedule E based on your rental use of the property. The remaining amount may be deductible as a personal itemized expense on Schedule A. If you paid $600 or more in interest on a mortgage during the year, the financial institution should send you a Form 1098 or similar statement by February showing the total interest you paid.

Line 13: Other interest

This is interest you paid to a lender other than a bank or other financial institution—for example, interest on a credit card you use for rental expenses.

Line 14: Repairs

Repairs keep your property in good working order. They do not add significant value to your property or extend its life. Do not include the cost of improvements in this line; they must be depreciated over several years. (See Chapter 6.)

Line 15: Supplies

This includes office supplies and supplies you use for repairs and maintenance—for example, paint and brushes, or fertilizer. It does not include materials you purchase to undertake improvements—for example, it would not include the cost of the shingles used to install a new roof on your rental property.

Line 16: Taxes

This includes the prorated amount of property taxes paid for the property based on the amount of rental use. Property tax you can't deduct as a rental expense may be deductible as an itemized personal deduction on Schedule A.

Line 17: Utilities

This includes charges for water, garbage pickup, gas, and electricity you pay for property. The amounts must be prorated based on your rental use of the property. Don't include utilities for a home office here.

Line 18: Depreciation

If you have multiple properties, you list your total depreciation deduction for each property in the depreciation line and then include the total for all properties on Line 23d. You must also complete and attach Form 4562, *Depreciation and Amortization (Including Information on Listed Property)*, if you are claiming:

- regular and bonus depreciation on property first placed in service during the year
- regular and bonus depreciation on listed property including a vehicle, regardless of the date it was placed in service, or
- a Section 179 expense deduction or amortization of costs that began during the year.

You should complete depreciation worksheets for each of your properties for which you claim depreciation, but you don't have to attach them to your return. (See Chapter 7 for a detailed discussion of depreciation.)

Line 19: Other expenses

Use the "Other" line to list other expenses not included in the above categories. You can deduct any expense for your rental activity that is ordinary and necessary. This includes:

- personal property items that cost $2,500 or less deducted under the de minimis safe harbor
- home office expenses
- gifts
- homeowners' association dues for condominiums and planned-unit developments
- start-up expenses

- registration or license fees for your short-term rental activity
- if you receive payment through PayPal or a similar online payment service, the fees the service charges
- the cost of purchasing a lockbox or having duplicate keys made
- the cost of storing your belongings while guests are staying in your home
- the cost of any credit reports you obtain in order to screen potential guests
- dues and subscriptions for your rental activity
- casualty losses, and
- equipment rental.

These expenses are all discussed in detail in Chapter 5.

Line 20: Total expenses

Add up all your expenses and put the total in Line 20.

Lines 21–26: Rental Summary

You use this portion of Schedule E to show the amount of income you earned or loss you incurred from your rental activity, and the deductible portion of any loss.

- **Line 21.** You complete this line only if you have rental losses all or part of which are not deductible because of the at-risk rules. If this is the case, you need to complete IRS Form 6198, *At-Risk Limitations*, and attach it to your return. You may only deduct losses up to the amount you are at risk. You are at risk for the total amount of any cash, property, or money you borrow to purchase your real property. Thus, very few hosts are affected by the at-risk limitations. See IRS Publication 925, *Passive Activity and At-Risk Rules*, for detailed guidance on the at risk rules.

- **Line 22.** If you're not subject to the vacation home rules (see below), you may be able to deduct all or part of your loss from other nonrental income. You may be able to deduct up to $25,000 in losses by using the $25,000 offset. If so, you don't need to file Form 8582, *Passive Activity Loss Limitations*. If you can't deduct your losses by using the offset, your losses will be deductible only if you're a real estate professional and materially participate in your rental activity. You'll have to complete Form 8582 to figure the amount of loss you can deduct, if any. Enter the deductible amount of your loss, if any, on Line 22. (See "Regular Rental Activity Rules," in Chapter 12, for more on deducting your rental losses.)

- **Lines 23a-23e.** You list here the total income, mortgage interest expense, depreciation, and total expenses for all your rental properties. If you only have one property, the amounts will be the same as shown in Column A.
- **Line 24 (Income).** Add any positive amounts shown on Line 21. Do not include any losses.
- **Line 25 (Losses).** Add royalty losses from Line 21 (if any) and rental losses from Line 22. Most hosts have no royalty losses.
- **Line 26 (Total income or loss).** Combine Lines 24 and 25. If there are no other entries on Schedule E, this amount is transferred to Line 17 of Form 1040. Otherwise, it is combined with other amounts on Line 41, Page 2, Schedule E.
- **Line 43 (Reconciliation for Real Estate Professionals).** If you're exempt from the passive activity loss rules because you are a real estate professional and materially participated in the rental activity, enter here the total profit or loss from all rental real estate rental activities.

Completing Schedule E When You Have a Rental Loss

You need to follow special rules to complete your Schedule E if you have a rental loss for the year and you're subject to the vacation home rules. You have a loss if all your deductible expenses for the year exceed your rental income. You are subject to the vacation home rules if you personally used the property you rented for the greater of 14 days or

10% of the rental days (if you personally used the property 34 or more days you'll always be subject to the vacation home rules). Most short-term rental hosts are subject to the vacation home rules, which apply not just to vacation homes, but to any home you both live in and rent out. These rules are covered in detail in Chapter 3.

When you have a loss and are subject to the vacation home rules, you may deduct no more than your gross rental income limitation for the year, which is your total rental income for the year minus:

- the rental portion of mortgage interest, real estate taxes, and any deductible casualty losses you incurred, and
- the full amount of direct rental expenses not related to the use of the home itself.

To avoid deducting too much, you must deduct your expenses from your rental income in a specific order on Schedule E. Use the following five-step approach to complete the expenses portion of Schedule E.

Step 1: List in Line 12 the allocable amount of your mortgage interest (plus deductible private mortgage insurance), list in Line 16 your deductible real estate taxes, and then list the amount of any deductible casualty losses in Line 19. You list only the prorated amounts for these expenses based on your rental use of the property.

Step 2: Next, list the full amounts of your direct rental expenses— these are expenses you incur specifically for your rental activity such as rental platform fees or travel expenses. These expenses vary from host to host. They may include, but are not limited to:

- rental platform fees and commissions you paid (Line 8)
- advertising (Line 5)
- auto and travel (Line 6)
- legal and other professional fees (Line 10)
- management fees (Line 11)
- short-term rental registration or licensing fees (Line 19)
- credit report fees (Line 19)
- home office deduction (Line 19), and
- depreciation for office furniture or equipment you use for your rental activity (Line 18).

Step 3: Add together all the expenses you've listed in Steps 1 and 2. Subtract the total from your rental income listed in Line 3. The difference is your gross rental income limitation for the year. Your deductions for all your other expenses cannot exceed this amount. If this is a positive number, go on to Step 4. If not, STOP: You can take no more deductions this year.

Step 4: If you have rental income left, deduct your operating expenses for the home, such as repairs (Line 14), utilities (Line 17), insurance (Line 9), cleaning and maintenance (Line 7), and supplies (Line 15). If you run out of income, STOP. No more expenses are deductible. If your total operating expenses exceed your gross rental income limitation, you are free to choose which to list on Schedule E. If you have income left after deducting all your operating expenses, continue to Step 5.

Step 5: Finally, deduct the allocable amount of your depreciation up to the amount of income remaining (Line 18).

Any amounts you can't deduct may be carried forward to future years and may be deductible then. You don't list these undeductible expenses on this Schedule E or anywhere else on your tax return. Just keep a record of them to use when you complete your Schedule E next year.

The IRS has created a helpful worksheet you can use to figure out your deductions to complete Schedule E. See Worksheet 5-1, contained in IRS Publication 527, *Residential Rental Property* (see below; this, and all other IRS publications can be downloaded at www.irs.gov). (Note, however, that the rental use percentage part of this worksheet (Part I) does not use the *Bolton* method to allocate expenses for mortgage interest and property tax—it can be advantageous for you to use the *Bolton* method; see Chapter 5.)

> EXAMPLE: This year, Rick used his vacation home that he purchased in 2015 for 30 days and rented the entire home to tourists through Airbnb for 90 days. His rental use percentage is 25% (30 ÷ 120 = .25). He incurred a $5,000 rental loss for the year: His total rental income

Worksheet 5-1, from IRS Publication 527, *Residential Rental Property*

Worksheet 5-1. **Worksheet for Figuring Rental Deductions for a Dwelling Unit Used as a Home**

Keep for Your Records

Use this worksheet only if you answer "yes" to all of the following questions.
- Did you use the dwelling unit as a home this year? (See *Dwelling Unit Used as a Home*.)
- Did you rent the dwelling unit at a fair rental price 15 days or more this year?
- Is the total of your rental expenses and depreciation more than your rental income?

PART I. Rental Use Percentage

A. Total days available for rent at fair rental price	**A.** _____
B. Total days available for rent (line A) but not rented	**B.** _____
C. **Total days of rental use.** Subtract line B from line A	**C.** _____
D. **Total days of personal use** (including days rented at less than fair rental price)	**D.** _____
E. **Total days of rental and personal use.** Add lines C and D	**E.** _____
F. **Percentage of expenses allowed for rental.** Divide line C by line E	**F.** . _____

PART II. Allowable Rental Expenses

1. Enter rents received		**1.** _____
2a. Enter the rental portion of deductible home mortgage interest and qualified mortgage insurance premiums (see instructions)	**2a.** _____	
b. Enter the rental portion of real estate taxes	**b.** _____	
c. Enter the rental portion of deductible casualty and theft losses (see instructions)	**c.** _____	
d. Enter direct rental expenses (see instructions)	**d.** _____	
e. **Fully deductible rental expenses.** Add lines 2a–2d. Enter here and on the appropriate lines on Schedule E (see instructions)		**2e.** _____
3. Subtract line 2e from line 1. If zero or less, enter -0-		**3.** _____
4a. Enter the rental portion of expenses directly related to operating or maintaining the dwelling unit (such as repairs, insurance, and utilities)	**4a.** _____	
b. Enter the rental portion of excess mortgage interest and qualified mortgage insurance premiums (see instructions)	**b.** _____	
c. Carryover of operating expenses from 2015 worksheet	**c.** _____	
d. Add lines 4a–4c	**d.** _____	
e. **Allowable expenses.** Enter the **smaller** of line 3 or line 4d (see instructions)		**4e.** _____
5. Subtract line 4e from line 3. If zero or less, enter -0-		**5.** _____
6a. Enter the rental portion of excess casualty and theft losses (see instructions)	**6a.** _____	
b. Enter the rental portion of depreciation of the dwelling unit	**b.** _____	
c. Carryover of excess casualty and theft losses and depreciation from 2015 worksheet	**c.** _____	
d. Add lines 6a–6c	**d.** _____	
e. **Allowable excess casualty and theft losses and depreciation.** Enter the **smaller** of line 5 or line 6d (see instructions)		**6e.** _____

PART III. Carryover of Unallowed Expenses to Next Year

7a. **Operating expenses to be carried over to next year.** Subtract line 4e from line 4d		**7a.** _____
b. **Excess casualty and theft losses and depreciation to be carried over to next year.** Subtract line 6e from line 6d		**b.** _____

was $15,000 and he had $20,000 in total deductible rental expenses. Because of the amount of rental and personal use, his rental activity is subject to the vacation home rules, which severely limit his ability to deduct his loss from other nonrental income. He must also follow the vacation home rules when he completes his Schedule E.

He incurred the following deductible rental expenses:

Rental Expense (prorated where required)	Amount
Mortgage interest	$6,000
Property tax	$1,500
Direct rental expenses (Airbnb fees, car expenses, registration fees)	$3,000
Operating expenses for home (utilities, cleaning and maintenance, repairs, supplies)	$5,000
Depreciation	$4,500
Total	$20,000

Rick's gross rental income limitation is $4,500 ($15,000 − ($6,000 + $1,500 + $3,000) = $4,500). He may only deduct $4,500 of his $5,000 in operating expenses for his home and none of his depreciation. He must carry forward $500 of operating expenses and $4,500 depreciation to future years. He may also deduct the personal use portion of his mortgage interest ($18,000) and property tax ($4,500) as an itemized deduction on IRS Schedule A. (Note that for 2018 through 2025, the itemized deduction for property tax is limited to $10,000; this limit does affect Rick.) Rick used the *Bolton* method to figure his mortgage interest and property tax deductions. This gave him a larger itemized deduction for these expenses than the IRS method because personal use is based on 365 days, not the 120 days the home was actually used by him and his guests. Had he used the IRS method, his mortgage interest rental expense would have been $18,000 instead of $6,000 and his property tax rental expense would have been $4,500.

Rick completes his Schedule E as follows:

Sample Schedule E (Form 1040)—page 1

SCHEDULE E
(Form 1040 or 1040-SR)

Department of the Treasury
Internal Revenue Service (99)

Supplemental Income and Loss
(From rental real estate, royalties, partnerships, S corporations, estates, trusts, REMICs, etc.)
► Attach to Form 1040, 1040-SR, 1040-NR, or 1041.
► Go to *www.irs.gov/ScheduleE* for instructions and the latest information.

OMB No. 1545-0074
2019
Attachment
Sequence No. **13**

Name(s) shown on return | Your social security number

Part I **Income or Loss From Rental Real Estate and Royalties** Note: If you are in the business of renting personal property, use Schedule C (see instructions). If you are an individual, report farm rental income or loss from **Form 4835** on page 2, line 40.

A Did you make any payments in 2019 that would require you to file Form(s) 1099? (see instructions) . . . . ☑ Yes ☐ No
B If "Yes," did you or will you file required Forms 1099? . . . . ☑ Yes ☐ No

1a Physical address of each property (street, city, state, ZIP code)
A 123 Main St. Anytown, ST 00000
B
C

1b	Type of Property (from list below)	2 For each rental real estate property listed above, report the number of fair rental and personal use days. Check the **QJV** box only if you meet the requirements to file as a qualified joint venture. See instructions.		Fair Rental Days	Personal Use Days	QJV
A	1		A	90	30	☐
B			B			☐
C			C			☐

Type of Property:
1 Single Family Residence   3 Vacation/Short-Term Rental   5 Land   7 Self-Rental
2 Multi-Family Residence   4 Commercial   6 Royalties   8 Other (describe)

Income:	Properties:		A	B	C
3	Rents received	3	15,000		
4	Royalties received	4			
Expenses:					
5	Advertising	5			
6	Auto and travel (see instructions)	6	2,000		
7	Cleaning and maintenance	7	1,000		
8	Commissions.	8	800		
9	Insurance	9			
10	Legal and other professional fees	10			
11	Management fees	11			
12	Mortgage interest paid to banks, etc. (see instructions)	12	6,000		
13	Other interest.	13			
14	Repairs.	14	2,800		
15	Supplies	15	200		
16	Taxes	16	1,500		
17	Utilities	17	500		
18	Depreciation expense or depletion	18			
19	Other (list) ► _____	19	200		
20	Total expenses. Add lines 5 through 19	20	15,000		
21	Subtract line 20 from line 3 (rents) and/or 4 (royalties). If result is a (loss), see instructions to find out if you must file **Form 6198**	21			
22	Deductible rental real estate loss after limitation, if any, on **Form 8582** (see instructions)	22 (	)(	)(	)

23a	Total of all amounts reported on line 3 for all rental properties	23a	15,000	
b	Total of all amounts reported on line 4 for all royalty properties	23b		
c	Total of all amounts reported on line 12 for all properties	23c	6,000	
d	Total of all amounts reported on line 18 for all properties	23d		
e	Total of all amounts reported on line 20 for all properties	23e	15,000	
24	**Income.** Add positive amounts shown on line 21. **Do not** include any losses	24	0
25	**Losses.** Add royalty losses from line 21 and rental real estate losses from line 22. Enter total losses here .	25 (	0)
26	**Total rental real estate and royalty income or (loss).** Combine lines 24 and 25. Enter the result here. If Parts II, III, IV, and line 40 on page 2 do not apply to you, also enter this amount on Schedule 1 (Form 1040 or 1040-SR), line 5, or Form 1040-NR, line 18. Otherwise, include this amount in the total on line 41 on page 2	26	0

For Paperwork Reduction Act Notice, see the separate instructions.   Cat. No. 11344L   Schedule E (Form 1040 or 1040-SR) 2019

Hosts Who Don't File Schedule E

There are certain situations where short-term rental hosts fall under different rules and have different filing requirements for reporting their rental income. Specifically, if you own or use your rental property in one of the following manners, you do not use Schedule E to report rental income or deductions for the property:

- You provide your guests with substantial services.
- You're married and elect qualified joint venture status.
- You're married, live in a community property state, and elect to treat your rental activity as a sole proprietorship.
- You operate your rental activity through a business entity such as a limited liability company.
- Your rental activity is a not-for-profit activity.

Hosts Who Provide Guests Substantial Services

Some hosts provide their guests with services similar to those provided by hotels or bed and breakfast establishments, such as meals and daily maid service. If such services are substantial, your activity is classified as a regular business, not a rental activity. (See Chapter 4.) In this event, do not file Schedule E. If you are an individual owner or the owner of a one-person LLC, file IRS Schedule C, *Profit or Loss From Business (Sole Proprietorship)*. Co-owners who are not spouses may form a business entity like an LLC to own the property; if not, they'll automatically be partners in a general partnership. Filing requirements for the different types of business entities are covered below.

Electing Qualified Joint Venture Status

Spouses who jointly own the property and provide significant personal services to their guests are also considered to be partners in a partnership, unless they form a different entity such as an LLC.

However, spouses have an option not available to other co-owners of property. Married couples (including same-sex couples) may elect to be taxed as a "qualified joint venture." If they qualify for the election, they are treated as sole proprietors for tax purposes and each spouse files a separate Schedule C reporting his or her share of rental income and expenses. This does not reduce their taxes, but it does result in a much simpler tax return because it won't be necessary to file a separate partnership tax return. Additionally, each spouse will receive separate credit for their Social Security and Medicare payments.

To qualify for qualified joint venture status, the spouses must share all their rental income, losses, deductions, and credits according to their ownership interest in the property. If, as is usually the case, each spouse owns 50% of the property, they equally split their rental income or loss on their Schedules C.

In addition, the spouses must:

- be the only owners of the activity
- file a joint return
- both elect not to be treated as a partnership, and
- both materially participate in the business (see "Hotel Business Rules," in Chapter 12, for an overview of material participation).

Spouses in Community Property States

Spouses who live in one of the nine states that have community property laws (Arizona, California, Idaho, Louisiana, Nevada, New Mexico, Texas, Washington, and Wisconsin) have yet another option: They may treat their rental activity as a sole proprietorship (technically, a "disregarded entity") and file one Schedule C in the name of one spouse. They do not need to elect qualified joint venture status to avoid having to file a partnership return. (Rev. Proc. 2002-69 (10/9/2002).)

Ownership Through a Business Entity

Real property owners always have the option of forming a business entity to own their property, instead of owning it in their own names as individuals. This is common for traditional residential landlords, especially those who own many rental units. Although few people do this when they rent out their main home to short-term guests, some people form business entities to own second or vacation homes.

The most popular business form for rental property ownership is the limited liability company (LLC). Other forms that can be used include general partnerships, limited partnerships, and corporations (usually, S corporations). If two or more people (other than spouses) own property together and don't form a separate entity, they automatically become partners in a general partnership. All these forms are "pass-through entities" —that is, they pay no tax themselves, instead all of their profits or losses are passed through the entity to their owners' individual tax returns.

If you form an LLC with only one owner, you file Schedule E, Part I, just like individual owners. This is because a single-owner LLC is a "disregarded entity" for tax purposes—it's as if it doesn't exist.

General and limited partnerships, multimember LLCs, and S corporations must all file annual tax returns with the IRS. Partnerships and most multimember LLCs file Form 1065, *U.S. Return of Partnership Income*. S corporations file Form 1120-S, *U.S. Income Tax Return for an S Corporation*. They must include with their returns IRS Form 8825, *Rental Real Estate Income and Expenses of a Partnership or an S Corporation*, to report rental income and deductions. This form is very similar to Schedule E. Individual LLC or partnership members (or S corporation shareholders) are each given a Schedule K-1 by the entity reporting their individual shares of annual income or loss from the rental activity. The individuals then list this amount on Part II of Schedule E, on Page 2.

Not-for-Profit Real Property Owners

If your rental activity constitutes a not-for-profit activity for tax purposes, you are not allowed to deduct any of your expenses starting in 2018 through 2025. Thus, you need not file Schedule E, Schedule A, or any other form listing them. However, you are still required to report and pay tax on the income you earned from your activity in the "Other income" line of Form 1040.

Tax-Free Home Rentals

Your rental activity is tax free if you rent the property involved for less than 15 days a year and use it personally for (1) more than 14 days, or (2) more than 10% of the rental days, whichever is greater. You don't need to file Schedule E or any other tax form for tax-free rentals. (See Chapter 3.) ●

Filing IRS Form 1099 Information Returns

This chapter explains when short-term rental hosts have their rental income reported to the IRS by others. It also shows when hosts themselves must file forms with the IRS to report payments they make to others in the course of their rental activity. These IRS Form 1099 filings are known as "information returns" because they provide information to the IRS on payments made to others. These tax filings help the IRS verify that the people receiving the payments reported on the Form 1099s report that same income on their own tax returns.

When Someone Else Reports Your Rental Income to the IRS

Traditional long-term residential landlords are typically paid rent by check or cash. These rental payments are almost never reported to the IRS (except when collected by a property management company). This is not necessarily the case, however, for short-term rental hosts. Hosts who list their rentals through short-term rental platforms like Airbnb are usually paid electronically, not by check or cash. The companies that process these payments have to report them to the IRS—but only if they exceed a certain dollar amount and transaction number threshold. Because the thresholds are high, most short-term rental hosts escape this reporting requirement.

Electronic payments. The IRS requires that electronic payment processors, such as PayPal, report the gross earnings of U.S. customers who earn over $20,000 and have more than 200 transactions in the calendar year.

The reporting is done by filing IRS Form 1099-K, *Payment Card and Third Party Network Transactions*. Copies of the form are sent by the processing company to the host, the IRS, and the host's state tax department. The deadline for filing with the host is January 31 of the year following the year the payments were made (the form is filed with the IRS and states by April 1).

When you list your property through Airbnb, VRBO (and other commission-based rental platforms), your guests pay Airbnb (or the other platform), which then pays you. Airbnb and VRBO issue a 1099-K to hosts located in the United States who have earned over $20,000 and had more than 200 reservations in a calendar year. Since the average host only earns about $7,500 per year and has far fewer than 200 transactions, such rental income usually doesn't get reported on 1099-K forms.

It's important to remember that even though most short-term rental hosts won't have their rental income reported to the IRS on a Form 1099-K, this income should be reported by the hosts on their annual tax return (see Chapter 10). The only exception is if your rental activity is tax free. If you're audited, the IRS can obtain your payment records from a credit card company or Airbnb or any other platform.

If you are issued a 1099-K, it will list the total amount of money processed for you during the year by the credit card company, Airbnb, or other rental platform, not the net amount you actually received. For example, there will be no deductions for host fees, refunds, or disputed credit card charges. You must list the total amount shown on the 1099-K as rental income on the appropriate tax form (Schedule E or C) and then deduct hosting fees and other expenses to arrive at your net taxable rental income.

Lower State Thresholds for Filing Form 1099-K

Most states require that a 1099-K be filed with the state income tax agency only if the form is also filed with the IRS. However, Massachusetts and Vermont have lower thresholds for filing Form 1099-K. These states require that a 1099-K be filed if a host is paid over $600 during the year. If your gross transaction value exceeds the state threshold, but falls below the federal threshold ($20,000 and 200 transactions), Airbnb and VRBO will file a form with the appropriate state agency only.

Reporting Payments You Make to ICs and Other Workers

If you hire people like cleaners, gardeners, or repair people to help you with your rental activity and pay them $600 or more during the year, you should be sure to report the payments to the IRS on IRS Form 1099-NEC (before 2020, Form 1099-MISC was filed instead of Form 1099-NEC). There are two important reasons to do so: First, failure to do this can result in monetary penalties by the IRS. Second, the filing of all required 1099s is an important factor the IRS considers when determining whether a rental activity is a business. You want your short-term rental activity to qualify as a business because you'll be able to take more deductions, including the pass-through deduction that can reduce the tax due on your rental income by as much as 20%.

Workers Subject to Reporting Requirement

You only need to report payments you make to independent contractors (ICs) you hire to help you with your rental activity. These are people running their own businesses, not your employees.

Moreover, you need not report payments you make to corporations. For example, if you hire a roofer named John James to fix your roof and pay $1,000 to him as an individual, the reporting requirement applies. But if you hire John James, Inc., to fix your roof, and pay $1,000 to his corporation, you need not report the payment.

$600 Threshold for Reporting

The 1099 filing requirement applies only if you pay an unincorporated independent contractor $600 or more during a year by check, cash, or direct deposit for rental-related services. It makes no difference whether the sum was one payment for a single job or the total of many small payments for multiple jobs.

In calculating whether the payments made to an independent contractor total $600 or more during a year, you must include payments you make for parts or materials the independent contractor used in performing the services. For example, if you hire an electrician to rewire your vacation home, and he charges you separately for the electrical wiring and other materials he installs, the cost must be included in the tally.

If payments to contractors include money for work performed for your rental activity and work not for your rental activity, you must prorate the amounts. Only if the prorated amount for your rental activity is $600 or more do you need to file a Form 1099-NEC. See Chapter 9 for details on how to prorate such payments.

> **EXAMPLE:** Jean pays Arthur $200 per month during the year to provide housecleaning services for her home. She rented the home through Airbnb for a total of four months during the year, thus she paid Arthur $800 for her short-term rental activity. She must report this amount on Form 1099-NEC.

Exception for Electronic and Credit Card Payments

You need not file a 1099-NEC if you pay an independent contractor:

- through a third-party settlement organization (TPSO) like PayPal or Payable
- by credit card, or
- by debit card.

This is true even if you paid the independent contractor over $600 during the year. The IRS requires TPSOs like PayPal to file Form 1099-K to report payments made to independent contractors who earn over $20,000 and have more than 200 transactions in the calendar year. But this is not your responsibility. Not having to file 1099-NEC forms relieves you of a bookkeeping burden. Independent contractors like it too because the IRS knows less about their income. So you'll only have to file a 1099-NEC if you pay more than $600 to an independent contractor by check, cash, or direct deposit.

Filing IRS Form 1099-NEC

You report your payments by filing IRS Form 1099-NEC with:

- the IRS
- your state tax department, and
- the independent contractor.

You can have an accountant or bookkeeper do this for you. However, it is not difficult to complete and fill out 1099-NEC forms yourself. One way is to order the official IRS 1099-NEC forms (which are scannable) from the IRS (you can't photocopy or download this multipart form from the IRS website). Go to www.irs.gov/businesses/online-ordering-for-information-returns-and-employer-returns. You can also use tax preparation or accounting software to prepare your 1099-NECs. Alternatively, there are inexpensive online services you can use to complete and file the forms.

Form 1099-NEC Replaces Old Form 1099-MISC

Until 2020, IRS Form 1099-MISC was used to report payments to independent contractors. Starting in 2021, new IRS Form 1099-NEC must be used for such payments. In 2021, it is used to report payments made to contractors in 2020. Form 1099-MISC was revised by the IRS and continues to be used to report other types of payments. Form 1099-NEC is used only for payments to nonemployees.

Filing Electronically

You have the option of filing 1099-NEC with the IRS electronically. However, you must provide a paper copy of the 1099-NEC form to the IC unless he or she agrees to accept an electronic 1099-NEC form. Unfortunately, you can't simply go on the IRS website, fill out a1099-NEC form online, and file it electronically. You must use software that meets IRS requirements. If you wish to file electronically yourself, you have three options:

Form 1099-NEC

7171	☐ VOID	☐ CORRECTED			

PAYER'S name, street address, city or town, state or province, country, ZIP or foreign postal code, and telephone no.

OMB No. 1545-0116

20**20**

Form **1099-NEC**

Nonemployee Compensation

1 Nonemployee compensation
$

2

Copy A
For
Internal Revenue
Service Center

File with Form 1096.

PAYER'S TIN | RECIPIENT'S TIN

RECIPIENT'S name

3

For Privacy Act
and Paperwork
Reduction Act
Notice, see the
**2020 General
Instructions for
Certain
Information
Returns.**

Street address (including apt. no.)

4 Federal income tax withheld
$

City or town, state or province, country, and ZIP or foreign postal code

FATCA filing requirement ☐

Account number (see instructions)

2nd TIN not. ☐

5 State tax withheld
$
$

6 State/Payer's state no.

7 State income
$
$

Form **1099-NEC**   Cat. No. 72590N   www.irs.gov/Form1099NEC   Department of the Treasury - Internal Revenue Service

Do Not Cut or Separate Forms on This Page — Do Not Cut or Separate Forms on This Page

- You can use accounting software such as *QuickBooks* or *Xero*.
- You can use online 1099-NEC filing services like efilemyforms. com, efile4biz.com, tax1099.com, and efile1099now.com.
- You can electronically file 1099-NEC forms directly with the IRS yourself by using its FIRE Production System. To do so, you must get permission from the IRS by filing IRS Form 4419, *Application for Filing Information Returns Electronically* (*FIRE*). This form need only be filed one time, and can be filed online. You must obtain a Transmitter Control Code (TCC) from the IRS, and create a user ID, password, and ten-digit PIN for your account. For more details, visit the IRS Filing Information Returns Electronically (FIRE) webpage at www.irs.gov/tax-professionals/e-file-providers-partners/filing-information-returns-electronically-fire.

Completing Form 1099-NEC

Filling out Form 1099-NEC is easy. Follow this step-by-step approach:

1. List your name, address, and telephone number in the first box titled PAYER'S name.

2. Enter your taxpayer identification number in the box entitled PAYER'S TIN.

3. The independent contractor you have paid is called the "RECIPIENT" on this form, meaning the person who received the money. Provide the independent contractor's taxpayer identification number (TIN), name, and address in the boxes indicated. For sole proprietors, you list the individual's name first, and then you may list a different business name, though this is not required. You may not enter only a business name for a sole proprietor.

4. Enter the amount of your payments to the independent contractor in Box 1, entitled Nonemployee Compensation.

5. If you've done backup withholding for an independent contractor who has not provided you with a taxpayer ID number, enter the amount withheld in Box 4.

6. Finally, if you withheld state tax from the IC's compensation, show the amount withheld in Box 6, your state tax ID number in Box 6, and the IC's total pay in Box 7. You may have to withhold state tax if you fail to get an IC's tax ID number or if you treat an IC as an employee for state tax purposes but not for federal tax purposes.

Form 1099-NEC contains five copies. These must be filed as follows:

- Copy A, the top copy, must be filed with the IRS no later than January 31 of the year after payment was made to the independent contractor. If you don't use the remaining two spaces for other independent contractors, leave those spaces blank. Don't cut the page.

- Copy 1 must be filed with your state taxing authority if your state has a state income tax. The filing deadline may be January 31 or it could be February 28 (which was the deadline for the IRS and most states before 2017), but check with your state tax department to make sure. Your state may also have a specific transmittal form or cover letter you must obtain.

- Copy B and Copy 2 must be given to the worker no later than January 31 of the year after payment was made.
- Copy C is for you to retain for your files.
- File all the IRS copies of each 1099-NEC form together with Form 1096, the simple transmittal form. Add up all the payments reported on all the 1099-NEC forms and list the total in the box indicated on Form 1099. File the forms with the IRS Service Center listed on the reverse of Form 1099.

Backup Withholding for Independent Contractors

Some independent contractors work in the underground economy— that is, they're paid in cash and never pay any taxes or file tax returns. The IRS may not even know they exist. The IRS wants you to help it find these people by supplying the taxpayer ID numbers from all independent contractors who meet the requirements explained above.

If an independent contractor won't give you his or her number or the IRS informs you that the number the independent contractor gave you is incorrect, the IRS assumes the person isn't going to voluntarily pay taxes. So it requires you to withhold taxes from the compensation you pay the independent contractor and remit them to the IRS. This is called backup withholding. If you fail to backup withhold, the IRS will impose an assessment against you equal to 24% of what you paid the independent contractor.

Backup withholding can be a bookkeeping burden for you. For- tunately, it's very easy to avoid it. Have the independent contractor fill out and sign IRS Form W-9, *Request for Taxpayer Identification Number and Certification*, and retain it in your files. (You can download it from the IRS website at www.irs.gov.) You don't have to file the W-9 with the IRS. This simple form merely requires the IC to list his or her name and address and taxpayer ID number. ●

Deducting Losses for Short-Term Rentals

Y ou need to read this chapter only if your short-term rental activity loses money—that is, your tax-deductible expenses exceed your rental income for the year. Losing money is never fun, but you may be able to deduct at least some or your losses from nonrental income you earned during the year. Unfortunately for short-term rental hosts, you need to apply exceedingly complex rules to determine if and how you can deduct any rental losses from your other income.

What Are Rental Losses?

Your short-term rental activity incurs a loss for tax purposes if all your deductions exceed the annual rent you receive from the property. If you own multiple properties, the annual income or losses from each property are combined (netted) to determine if you have income or loss from all your rental activities for the year. Obviously, you can't know if you have a loss until you total all your deductions and subtract them from your rental income. It's not uncommon for people who rent real estate to have losses for tax purposes. Often, you have a loss for tax purposes even if your rental income exceeds your operating expenses. This is because your depreciation deduction is included as an expense for these purposes. However, due to the coronavirus (COVID-19) pandemic, short-term rental occupancy rates plummeted by as much as 90% or more in many areas for many months. As a result, many short-term hosts experienced losses in 2020 for the first time.

> EXAMPLE: Allie ordinarily earns $12,000 per year renting her main home part-time through Airbnb. However, she earned only $1,000 in 2020 due to a massive number of cancellations caused by the coronavirus pandemic. Her total deductible rental expenses are listed below (note that most of these are prorated amounts based on the percentage of the time the home was rented; see Chapter 9).

Expense	Amount
Airbnb fees	$180
Cleaning and maintenance	$1,000
Insurance	$300
Repairs	$600
Supplies	$400
Mortgage interest	$2,000
Taxes	$1,000
Utilities	$500
Depreciation	$3,000
Total	$8,980

Allie incurred a $7,980 rental loss for 2020 ($8,980 expenses − $1,000 rental income = $7,980 rental loss). She earned $100,000 from her job during the year. Can she deduct her loss from this income and save over $1,000 in income tax? Read on.

Which Rental Loss Rules Apply

There are significant restrictions on the ability of rental property owners to deduct rental losses from other nonrental income. These restrictions are particularly severe for part-time rentals of property where the owner lives in the property most of the time. There are three different sets of rules:

- vacation home rules
- hotel business rules, and
- regular rental activity loss rules.

Which rules apply depends on how much of the time you live in the property, how much you rent it out, and whether you provide substantial services to your guests. These categories are summarized in the following chart.

Annual Rental Use	Annual Personal Use	Substantial Services Provided?	Which Rules Apply
More than 14 days	More than 14 days or more than 10% of rental days	n/a	Vacation home rules
More than 14 days	14 days or less, or no more than 10% of rental days	Yes	Hotel business rules
More than 14 days	14 days or less, or no more than 10% of rental days	No	Regular rental activity rules

Most short-term rental hosts must apply the vacation home rules. The other categories apply only where hosts make very limited personal use of the property.

Vacation Home Rules

The vacation home rules greatly restrict your ability to deduct losses from your main home, vacation home, or other property that you live in substantially more of the time than you rent it out to others. They apply to condos, co-ops, and apartments, as well as to single-family homes. They apply whether you rent your entire home part time, or only a room or rooms in your home. They also apply to any structures "appurtenant" to your home that don't contain basic living accommodations, such as sleeping space, toilet, and cooking facilities—for example, a garage. (I.R.C. § 280A-1(c)(2).)

These rules are confusingly called the "dwelling unit used as a home" or "dwelling unit used as a personal residence" rules by the IRS. We'll refer to them more simply as the vacation home rules. However, they apply to any type of property you both live in and rent out and they apply whether you own or rent your home. Moreover, they can apply to more than one property you own—for example, to both your main home and a vacation home.

Exception for Full-Time Room Rentals

The vacation home rules don't apply if you rent a room or rooms in your home full time. "Full time" means that the room or rooms are either occupied by paying guests or available for rent, and never used personally by you. In this event, the hotel business or regular rental activity rules apply to any losses you incur.

Personal Use Threshold

Your rental losses are subject to the vacation home rules if (1) you rent all or part of your home for more than 14 days during the year, and (2) you make personal use of your home for the greater of:

- more than 14 days, or
- more than 10% of the number of days the property is rented for a fair rental during the year. (I.R.C. § 280A(d)(2).)

Here's a simple shortcut: The vacation home rules will always apply if you make personal use of your home for 34 or more days during the year. They could also apply if your personal use is less than this amount.

> **EXAMPLE:** Paul rents his entire home through Airbnb for 65 days during the year and lives in it for 300 days (10% x 65 = 6.5). His 300 personal use days are more than the greater of 14 days or 6.5 days, so the vacation rule threshold is exceeded.

Personal use can include not just your own use of the property, but use by your relatives or friends as well. (See Chapter 9, for detailed guidance on how to calculate your rental and personal use days.)

Most short-term rental hosts live in the property they rent more than 34 days, so they are subject to the restrictive vacation home rules if they incur losses.

Limits on Deducting Losses

If your rental activity is subject to the vacation home rules, there are strict limits on deducting losses from nonrental income. The passive activity loss rules that normally apply to long-term residential rentals and that permit some landlords to deduct their losses do not apply here. Instead, you are permitted to deduct your expenses only up to the amount of your "gross rental income limitation." This is an important number. It is equal to your total rental income for the year minus the following expenses:

- the rental portion of mortgage interest, real estate taxes, and any deductible casualty losses you incurred, and
- the full amount of direct rental expenses not related to the use of the home itself.

Direct rental expenses include any expense you incur solely to rent your property to short-term guests. They don't include expenses to maintain or use the property itself like repairs, utilities, or cleaning expenses. For example, they can include Airbnb commissions, website and other advertising expenses, deductible car and travel expenses, short-term rental registration or licensing fees, depreciation for office furniture or equipment you use for your rental activity, office supplies, home office deduction, PayPal charges, credit report fees, and dues and subscriptions for your rental activity.

You may deduct all the above expenses in full even if they exceed your rental income for the year. However, all your other expenses, such as depreciation and utilities, are deductible only if, and to the extent, they don't exceed your gross rental income limitation.

> **EXAMPLE:** Assume you're subject to the vacation home rules and earned $10,000 renting your home through Airbnb this year. The rental portion of your mortgage interest was $5,000 and prorated property tax was $2,000. Your total direct operating expenses were $1,000. You may deduct these amounts in full from your rental income. After you do this, your gross rental income limitation is $2,000 ($10,000 − ($5,000 + $2,000 + $1,000) = $2,000). Thus, you may only deduct $1,000 of all the other expenses you incurred for your rental activity during the year.

Undeductible Losses Are Carried Forward

Any undeductible losses you have for the year can be carried forward to future years and deducted from your rental income from the property, if you have enough. You deduct them using the same three-step process for determining your gross rental income limitation described above (this is so even if you're not subject to the vacation home rules for the current year). In real life, however, these losses are rarely deducted in future years because the property usually does not generate enough income.

When the property is sold, there will no longer be rental income received from it, and any unused carryforward losses will simply disappear. The IRS has provided no guidance on whether you can use these carryforward losses to offset all or part of profit you earn from the sale. You should consult a tax professional if you want to do this.

Completing IRS Schedule E

If you're subject to the vacation home rules, you file IRS Schedule E to report your income and expenses. How to complete Schedule E is covered in Chapter 10. When the vacation home rules apply, you must follow strict ordering rules when calculating and reporting your deductions on Schedule E to ensure that you don't deduct too much.

You must deduct your expenses from your rental income in the following order:

- **Category 1 expenses.** These are the rental portion of your mortgage interest (plus deductible private mortgage insurance), real estate taxes, and any deductible casualty losses.
- **Category 2 expenses.** Fully deductible direct expenses incurred solely to rent the home, such as rental platform fees or travel expenses—these don't include expenses to operate or maintain your home.
- **Category 3 expenses.** The rental portion of operating expenses for the home include such things as repairs, utilities, insurance, maintenance, and cleaning.
- **Category 4 expenses.** These are the rental portion of depreciation for your home.

Subtract Category 1 and 2 expenses from your rental income. The difference is your gross rental income limitation for the year. Your deductions for Category 3 and 4 expenses cannot exceed this amount. Category 1 and 2 expenses can be deducted even if they exceed your rental income.

> EXAMPLE: This year, Rick used his mountain vacation home for 30 days and rented the entire home to tourists through Airbnb for 90 days. Based on the rental and personal days, he has a 75% rental allocation. His total expenses were $25,000 and his total rental income was $10,000. His rental activity is subject to the vacation home rules. He must deduct his expenses in the following order and amounts on Schedule E:

Expense	Amount	Amount Allocated to Rental Use	Amount Deducted	Remaining Rental Income	Unused Deduction
Mortgage interest	$10,000	$7,500 (75%)	$7,500	$2,500	0
Property tax	$2,000	$1,500 (75%)	$1,500	$1,000	0
Direct expenses	$750	$750 (100%)	$750	$250	0
Operating expense	$6,000	$4,500 (75%)	$250	0	$4,250
Depreciation	$6,250	$4,688 (75%)	0	0	$4,688
Total	$25,000	$18,938	$10,000	0	$8,938

> Rick may also deduct 25% of his property tax and mortgage interest as a personal itemized deduction on his Schedule A. This is the amount of taxes and rent allocated to the time he personally used the vacation home. This amounts to a $3,000 deduction. All in all, this is not a good result for Rick. He had $25,000 in expenses, but can deduct only $10,000. Because his gross rental income limitation was only $250, he has $8,938 in unused deductions he must carry forward to the next year, including $4,688 in depreciation.

Allocation Strategy to Increase Your Current Deduction

If, like in the above example, the property you rent is your main home or vacation home for which you can deduct mortgage interest and taxes as a personal deduction, you can increase your total deductions by increasing the amount of mortgage interest and property tax deducted as a personal itemized deduction on Schedule A. This way, more of your operating expenses and depreciation can be deducted from rental income. You can do this by using a different allocation formula for property taxes and interest.

Instead of using the number of days the property was actually used during the year to figure your rental percentage, you use 365 days (referred to as the "*Bolton* method"). This is not the way the IRS would like you to allocate these expenses, and you won't find a word about it in any IRS publication or regulation. However, the courts have approved it, reasoning that interest and property taxes are paid for an entire year, not just when a home is used. (*Bolton v. Comm'r*, 694 F.2d 556 (9th Cir. 1982); *McKinney v. Comm'r*, 732 F.2d 414 (10th Cir. 1983).) Thus, this is a permissible method for you to use.

If Rick used the *Bolton* method, his allocation percentage for his tax and interest would be 25% instead of 75% (90 ÷ 365 = 25%). Thus, Rick would deduct only $500 of his property tax and $2,500 of his interest from his $10,000 in rental income. Now, his gross rental income limitation is $6,000 instead of $250. This allows him to deduct an additional $6,000 in operating expenses and depreciation. He could deduct the other 75% of his taxes and interest as a $9,000 itemized deduction on his Schedule A. His Schedule E deductions would look like this:

Expense	Amount	Amount Allocated to Rental Use	Amount Deducted	Remaining Rental Income	Unused Deduction
Mortgage interest	$10,000	$2,500 (25%)	$2,500	$7,500	0
Property tax	$2,000	$500 (25%)	$500	$7,000	0
Direct expenses	$750	$750 (100%)	$750	$6,250	0
Operating expenses	$6,000	$4,500 (75%)	$4,500	$1,750	0
Depreciation	$6,250	$4,688 (75%)	$1,750	0	$2,938
Total	$25,000	$12,938	$10,000	$22,500	$2,938

If you use this method, you should do so consistently—that is, you should continue to do so every year you rent your property.

However, as a result of the Tax Cuts and Jobs Act, there are several instances where it is not advisable to use the *Bolton* method to figure your allocable mortgage interest.

Using the IRS method will give more mortgage interest to deduct as a rental expense. Thus, you'd be better off using the IRS method if you're unable to deduct the mortgage interest allocated to personal use on Schedule A as a personal itemized deduction. This would be the case, for example, if you are unable to itemize your deductions because the standard deduction exceeds your total itemized deductions. The Tax Cuts and Jobs Act roughly doubled the standard deduction. For 2020, the deduction is $12,400 for singles and $24,800 for married people filing jointly. The TCJA also eliminated many personal deductions for 2018 through 2025. As a result, many more hosts than ever before are unable to itemize their deductions because their mortgage interest, property tax, and other personal deductions (such as charitable contributions) don't exceed the standard deduction.

Even if you do itemize, the Tax Cuts and Jobs Act established new annual limits for the personal deduction for home mortgage interest and property tax. For 2018 through 2025, a total of $10,000 in property tax can be deducted each year for a main and second home. For main and second homes purchased December 15, 2017 through December 31, 2025, mortgage interest on only up to $750,000 in acquisition debt can be deducted as a personal itemized deduction. For homes purchased before December 15, 2017, interest payments on up to $1 million in acquisition debt may be deducted. Acquisition debt is money borrowed to buy, build or "substantially improve" a main home and a second home.

If either or both of these limitations prevent you from deducting part of your property tax and/or mortgage interest payments, you could be better off using the IRS method and claiming more mortgage interest as a rental expense. You should run the numbers both ways to decide which method to use. But, once you choose a method, you must stick with it. You can't switch back and forth whenever you feel like it.

Hotel Business Rules

Losses you incur from your rental activity are not subject to the vacation home rules discussed above if (1) you use the property involved for 14 days or less during the year, or (2) the days you personally use the property are equal to no more than 10% of the rental days—for example, you rent your vacation home for 90 days and use it personally for eight days, which is equal to 9% of the rental days.

Most hosts rent or live in their property too much to satisfy either of these criteria. But, if you do meet either test, the hotel business rules will likely apply. This is the case if either of the following applies:

- You rent to guests for an average period of seven days or less.
- Your average rental period is eight to 30 days and you provide "significant services" to your guests.

In this event, for purposes of deducting losses, your activity is not considered a rental activity. Instead, it's treated like a regular business—the same way hotels and bed and breakfast businesses are treated. This may or may not make it easier to deduct your losses; it all depends on how much time you spend on your rental activity.

Rentals for Seven Days or Less

For purposes of deducting losses, your rental activity is classified as a hotel business if the average period of rental use of your property is seven days or less. (IRS Reg. § 1.469-1T(e)(3)(ii)(A).) To determine the average period of rental use, you divide the total days your property was rented by the total number of stays. For example, if you rent your property to 20 guests during the year for a total of 100 days, your average period of rental use is 100 ÷ 20 = 5 days, and your activity is classified as a hotel business. Most short-term rental hosts rent their property no more than seven days on average to each guest.

Rentals for 30 Days or Less With Significant Services

If the average rental period is more than seven days but less than 30 days, your activity will still be classified as a hotel business if you provide "significant services" to your guests. Significant services do not include services commonly provided for high-grade residential rentals, such as repairs, cleaning, maintenance, trash removal, elevators, security, or cable television. (IRS Reg. 1.469-1T(e)(3)(iv)(B)(3).) Rather, they are hotel-like services provided for guests' convenience, not to maintain the property. Examples include:

- maid service
- meals or snacks
- laundry services
- concierge services
- transportation
- amenities like linens, irons, hangers, shampoo, and soap, or
- other hotel-like services.

IRS examples indicate that such services are significant only if their value is equal to at least more than 10% of the income received from the activity. However, in determining the value of services for these purposes, only services performed by individuals are counted. Thus, for example, services such as telephone and cable television service are not taken into account. (IRS Reg. 1.469-1T(e)(3)(ii).)

If you're providing significant services to your guests for purposes of the loss rules, you are also likely providing "substantial services" for purposes of Social Security and Medicare taxes and you should be filing Schedule C to report your income and expenses. (See Chapter 2.) "Substantial services" and "significant services" are not the same and are governed by separate provisions of the tax law, but they are similar. It's likely that if one applies the other does too.

Deducting Losses for Hotel Businesses

When the hotel business rules apply, you can deduct your losses from other nonrental income if you "materially participate" in the business. You materially participate in a business only if you are involved with its day-to-day operations on a regular, continuous, and substantial basis. (I.R.C. § 469(h).) The IRS has created seven tests to determine material participation, based on the amount of time you spend working in the business. You only need to pass one of the tests to show material participation. Most people use one or more of the following tests.

To determine the number of hours you participate in your rental activity, you may include the time your spouse puts in, but not your children.

500-hour test. You participated in the activity for more than 500 hours during the year.

Substantially all test. You did substantially all the work in the activity during the year. You don't have to do 100% of the work, but others may only do an insubstantial amount. You must include hours spent working on the property by co-owners, employees, and independent contractors, such as property managers. If others also work in the real estate activity along with you, you should have records showing how much time each person worked in the activity.

101-hour test. You participated in the business for more than 100 hours during the year, and you participated at least as much as any other person (including employees and independent contractors, such as property managers, cleaners, repair people).

Past performance test. You satisfy any of the IRS tests for material participation for any five of the last ten years. This test is rarely used.

> EXAMPLE: Lee owns a four bedroom house at a lake in the mountains. She rents out three bedrooms to tourists. This year, 30 guests stayed a total of 300 days, resulting in an average rental period of ten days. She lived in the house only 25 days, which was less than 10% of the rental days. After deducting all her expenses, Lee incurred a $5,000 loss from her rentals. Lee provided her guests with daily maid service, laundry service, breakfasts and snacks, and use of her boat. The value of these personal services exceeded 10% of the rent she charged, so she provided her guests with significant services. Her activity qualifies as a hotel business. Lee may deduct her loss from her nonrental income only if she materially participated in the activity during the year. Lee worked more than 100 hours at the activity during the year, which was more than anyone else. Thus, she materially participated and may deduct her $5,000 loss from her active or investment income.

It can be hard for many hosts to put in enough hours to materially participate in their short-term rental activity, especially if they're only renting a main home, or vacation home, for a few days a year. Consider the case of Charles Akers, who owned a three-bedroom cabin that he rented for 12 days in 2004 with an average guest stay of three days. He was not allowed to deduct his claimed $20,258 rental loss from his other income because he couldn't show he materially participated in his rental activity. He had no proof that he spent more than 100 hours engaged in the rental of the cabin. Nor could he show he spent more time working on the rental than anyone else. Indeed, this seemed unlikely since he hired a management company and cleaning service to help him with the rental. (*Akers v. Comm'r.*, T.C. Memo 2010-85.)

You should learn from Charles Akers's mistakes. Keep careful track of the actual number of hours you (and your spouse) spend working on your rental activity during the year. You can note your time on a calendar, appointment book, log, or timesheet. It doesn't matter, as long as your records are accurate and believable. This will help document your participation.

Grouping Multiple Properties

If you own multiple rental properties, you can group them together as one single activity. This way, you can combine the time you spend working on each rental property to satisfy the material participation tests. You generally can group short-term with long-term rental properties, if you own both. To do this, you file a statement called an election with your tax return. For details, see Chapter 16 of *Every Landlord's Tax Deduction Guide*, by Stephen Fishman (Nolo).

Suspended Passive Losses

If you don't materially participate, you can't deduct your rental losses from your other income you have for the year. However, these losses don't disappear. Instead, they become "suspended passive activity losses" that are carried forward indefinitely to future years. You may deduct them from passive income you earn in any future year—that is, rental income or income from other businesses in which you don't materially participate. You may also deduct such losses from any profit you earn when you sell the property to an unrelated party—that is, a person other than a relative.

No Personal Deduction for Mortgage Interest

When you personally use your home less than 14 days or less than 10% of the rental days, it is not considered your residence for purposes of deducting mortgage interest as a personal itemized deduction on IRS Schedule A. Thus, you may not deduct the amount of interest allocated to your personal use days. Instead this interest is nondeductible consumer interest. (I.R.C. § 163.)

> **EXAMPLE:** Rich rents his vacation home for 330 days and lives in it for 30 days, less than 10% of the rental days. He pays $1,000 per month in mortgage interest on the home. He may not deduct the 30 days of mortgage interest allocated to his personal use days.

Beware Not-for-Profit Rules

If you continually incur losses on your rental, the IRS could claim that your primary motive for renting it is something other than earning a profit. If your rental is deemed to be a not-for-profit activity, starting in 2018 through 2025, you will not be allowed to deduct your rental expenses from your rental income and you must pay tax on your income. You are never allowed to deduct any losses from a not-for-profit activity from your other nonrental income. To avoid the not-for-profit rules, you must show the IRS that you are serious about earning a profit from your rental activity. See Chapter 4 for a detailed discussion of the not-for-profit rules.

Regular Rental Activity Rules

Your short-term rental activity is subject to the regular rental activity rules if:

- you rent the property involved for more than 14 days, and live in it for 14 days or less or no more than 10% of the rental days; *and*

- your activity doesn't qualify as a hotel business as described above. This means your guests stay on average more than 30 days; or they stay at least eight to 30 days on average and you don't provide them with significant services.

If both requirements are met, for purposes of deducting losses your short-term rental activity is treated the same as a long-term residential rental. In other words, you're treated like a regular landlord.

> EXAMPLE: John owns a vacation cabin that he rented out 180 days during the year to 20 guests. Thus, his guests stayed an average of nine days. He used the cabin personally for 14 days, which was only equal to 8% of the rental days. He did not provide his guests with personal services. He had a $5,000 loss for the year from the rental activity. He must apply the regular rental activity rules to determine if he may deduct this loss from his other nonrental income.

When you have a regular rental activity, the tax code's passive activity loss rules apply. (I.R.C. § 469.) These are the rules that apply to deducting losses from long-term residential rentals. They are covered in exhaustive detail in Chapter 16 of *Every Landlord's Tax Deduction Guide*, by Stephen Fishman (Nolo). The two ways you can deduct your losses under these rules are described below.

The $25,000 Offset

The $25,000 offset permits landlords with relatively modest incomes to deduct up to $25,000 in rental losses each year. The offset applies to all rental properties you own—that is, you don't get a separate $25,000 for each property you own. (I.R.C. § 469(I).) To qualify for the offset, you must come within the income ceiling and actively participate in your rental activity. You must also own at least 10% of the property involved.

You're allowed to take full advantage of the $25,000 offset only if your modified adjusted gross income (MAGI) is less than $100,000. The deduction is phased out if your MAGI is more than $100,000—for every dollar your MAGI exceeds $100,000, you reduce your $25,000 offset by 50 cents. Thus, the offset is eliminated entirely once your MAGI exceeds $150,000. For most taxpayers, their MAGI is all of their income, not counting their rental income or loss.

Moreover, you qualify for the $25,000 offset only if you actively participate in the running of your rental activity. This is very easy to do. You don't have to work any set number of hours to actively participate; you simply have to be the person who makes the final decisions about approving tenants, arranging for repairs, setting rents, and other management tasks. If you manage your rentals yourself, you'll satisfy this requirement without any problem. The IRS probably won't even raise the issue if you're audited. Management tasks performed by your spouse are also counted in determining if you actively participate. (I.R.C. § 469(i)(6)(D).)

> **EXAMPLE:** Assume that John from the above example had a MAGI of $99,000, which includes $95,000 in salary from his job. He qualifies for the full $25,000 offset. This enables him to deduct his entire $5,000 short-term rental loss on his Form 1040. This reduces his taxable income by $5,000 and saves him $1,250 in federal income tax.

If you have more than $25,000 in annual losses, you don't lose the excess amount. Instead, they become suspended losses you can deduct the following year or years provided you qualify for the offset during those years. You can also deduct them when you sell the property.

Real Estate Professional Exemption

If you're a real estate professional, you can deduct all your losses from a regular rental activity from other nonrental income provided that you materially participate in the rental activity.

You're a real estate professional only if you spend at least 51% of your work time during the year working at one or more real property businesses in which you materially participate. You don't have to work solely as a host; other real estate businesses can count as well—for example, working as real estate broker or agent. You or your spouse must also spend at least 751 hours per year working at your real property business or businesses in which you materially participate. The same spouse must pass both the 751-hour and 51% tests.

If you qualify as a real estate professional, you may deduct all the losses you incur from a part-time rental activity from your nonrental income if you materially participate in that activity. You apply the material participation rules described above. To help you satisfy the material participation tests, you can group together your rental activities so that the hours you spend working on each of them can be combined. For a detailed discussion of the real estate professional exemption, see Chapter 16 of *Every Landlord's Tax Deduction Guide*, by Stephen Fishman (Nolo).

Annual Loss Limits

Depending on the year involved, there could be an annual limit on the total business losses you are allowed to deduct on your tax return. These limits apply whether your short-term rental activity qualifies as a hotel business or regular rental activity. The limits are quite high, so they don't affect most hosts.

Losses Before 2018

Before 2018, there were no annual dollar limits on deducting business or rental losses.

Losses Incurred 2018-2020

The Tax Cuts and Jobs Act established a new limit on deducting business losses by taxpayers other than regular C corporations, which affected the vast majority of rental property owners. As originally enacted, the TCJA provided that, starting in 2018 and continuing through 2025, single taxpayers could deduct no more than $250,000 per year in business losses, including rental business losses, over their rental and other business income. Married taxpayers filing jointly could deduct no more than $500,000. These numbers are adjusted for inflation—for 2019, the limits were $255,000/$510,000.

In other words, a host deducts losses equal to his or her total income from the rental business and any other businesses and an additional $250,000 or $500,000. The effect was that no more than $250,000/$500,000 in rental losses could be deducted from nonrental income in any one year during 2018 through 2025 (plus an amount for the inflation adjustment). Excess losses had to be deducted in future years as part of the taxpayer's net operating loss (NOL).

However, the CARES Act enacted in 2020 by Congress eliminated the annual limit for losses incurred during 2018 through 2020. Such losses are fully deductible (subject to the passive loss rules). Taxpayers who were unable to deduct part of their losses for 2018 or 2019, due to the limit, may amend their returns for the years involved to claim them.

Losses Incurred 2021-2025

Losses incurred during 2021 through 2025 are subject to an annual limit of $259,000 for singles and $518,000 for married taxpayers filing jointly. Unused losses—called "excess business losses"—will have to be deducted in future years as part of the taxpayer's net operating loss (NOL) carryforward.

Excess business losses are calculated as follows:
1. Add all your income for the year from all your businesses, rental and nonrental, plus wage income.
2. Add to this total $259,000 if single, $518,000 if married filing jointly—this is the total amount of losses you may deduct.
3. Subtract this amount from your total rental and other business losses for the year—any positive number is an excess business loss.

> EXAMPLE: Sheila, a single taxpayer, is a successful real estate broker who also owns multiple properties she rents out to short-term guests. She grouped together the properties for passive loss purposes. She qualifies as a real estate professional and materially participates in her rental activity. Thus, the passive loss rules don't prevent her from deducting her losses from her nonpassive income. In 2021, she earned $100,000 from her real estate brokerage business (and had no other income) and she had $400,000 in rental losses. Her excess business loss is $41,000 ($400,000 − (100,000 + $259,000) = $41,000).

If rental property is owned through a multimember LLC taxed as a partnership or an S corporation, the $259,000/$518,000 limit applies to each owner's or member's share of the pass-through's losses.

The limit applies after the passive loss rules are applied. Presumably, if a rental loss is disallowed under the passive loss rules, any deductions or income from the activity would not be considered in calculating an excess business loss.

The excess business loss limitation applies to the total (aggregate) income and deductions from all of a taxpayer's trades or businesses, including rental and nonrental businesses. If spouses filing jointly have separate businesses, the $518,000 limit applies to the total income and deductions from all of their businesses, rental and nonrental. ●

Record Keeping

Your deductions for your short-term rental expenses are only as good as the records you keep to back them up. Any deduction you forget to claim on your tax return, or lose after an IRS audit because you lack adequate records, costs you dearly. Every $100 in unclaimed deductions costs the average midlevel-income host in a 24% tax bracket an additional $24 in federal income taxes. This chapter shows you how to document your expenses and other deductions so you won't end up paying more tax than you have to.

What Records Do You Need?

If, like most small short-term rental hosts, you haven't formed a separate business entity to own your property and you have no employees, you need three types of records for tax purposes:

- a record of your rental income and expenses
- supporting documents for your income and expenses, and
- a record of how your property was used during the year.

You need records of your income and expenses to figure out whether your rental activity earned a taxable profit or incurred a deductible loss during the year. You'll also have to summarize your rental income and expenses for each rental property in your tax return (IRS Schedule E).

You need receipts and other supporting documents, such as credit card records, account statements, and canceled checks, to serve as insurance in case you're audited by the IRS. These supporting documents enable you to prove to the IRS that your claimed expenses are genuine. Some expenses—travel, for example—require particularly stringent documentation. Without this paper trail, you'll lose valuable deductions in the event of an audit. Remember, if you're audited, it's up to you to prove that your deductions are legitimate.

You need a record of how many days the property was rented, used personally, and vacant to allocate many of your expenses.

If you own more than one property you rent to short-term guests, you must track each property separately—don't mix them together. One reason for this inconvenient rule is that the IRS requires that you separately list your income and expenses for each property on your Schedule E. Also, you'll never know how much money you're making or losing on each property unless you separately track your income and expenses.

Separate Rental Bank Account

Although it's not mandatory, it's a good idea to set up a separate checking account for your rental activity. Your rental checkbook will serve as your basic source of information for recording your rental expenses and income. Deposit all of your rental income into the account and make rental-related payments from the account. If you're paid electronically— for example, through PayPal—have the payments deposited into this account. Don't use your rental account to pay for personal expenses or your personal account to pay for rental activity items.

Using a separate account will provide these important benefits:

- It will be much easier for you to keep track of your rental income and expenses if you pay them from a separate account.
- Your rental account will clearly separate your personal and rental activity finances; this will prove very helpful if the IRS audits you.
- Your rental account will help convince the IRS that your rental is a for-profit activity. People with not-for-profit activities don't generally have separate bank accounts to fund their pursuits. (See Chapter 4 for more on establishing your tax status.)

When you write rental activity checks, you may have to make some extra notations besides the date, number, amount of the check, and the name of the person or company to which the check is written. If the purpose of the payment is not clear from the name of the payee, describe the rental reason for the check—for example, the equipment or service you purchased.

Separate Credit Card for Rental Activity Expenses

Use a separate credit card for rental activity expenses instead of putting both personal and rental items on one card. Credit card interest for rental activity purchases is 100% deductible, while interest for personal purchases is not deductible at all. Using a separate card for rental-related purchases will also make it much easier for you to keep track of how much interest you've paid for these purchases. If you have more than one personal credit card, you can use one for your rental activity only—you don't need to get a special business credit card.

Tracking Income and Expenses

You should create an income and expense journal to keep track of what you earn from, and spend on, your short-term rental activity. There are various ways to do this. The IRS does not require you to use any particular method. You can keep your journal manually on paper; set up an electronic spreadsheet, such as *Excel* (you can download spreadsheet templates for this); use personal finance software such as *Quicken*; use more powerful accounting software, such as *QuickBooks*, or use software especially designed for landlords, such as *Quicken Rental Property Manager* or *Buildium*. There are also apps such as *Hurdlr* especially designed for use by short-term hosts. Use whatever method works best for you.

Rental Expenses

Keep track of your expenses in your journal by category. Your rental expense categories should be keyed to the categories on IRS Schedule E, the tax form you file to report your rental expenses and income. This is how the IRS wants you to categorize your expenses when you report them on your taxes, so you should use these categories in your records. This way, you simply transfer the totals from your records to your Schedule E when you do your taxes.

Schedule E lists 13 expense categories:
- advertising
- auto and travel
- cleaning and maintenance
- commissions
- insurance
- legal and other professional fees
- management fees
- mortgage interest paid to banks
- other interest
- repairs
- supplies
- taxes, and
- utilities.

The ins and outs of Schedule E are discussed in Chapter 10. Refer to that chapter if you need more information about these categories. You may not need to use all of these categories—for example, if you manage your rental activity by yourself, you probably don't need the management fees category.

The Schedule E categories probably include most of your expenses, but you may have others that are not listed—for example:
- home office expenses
- gifts
- homeowners' association dues for rental condominiums and planned-unit developments
- amenities you purchase for your guests
- storage costs for your personal items when you rent
- start-up expenses
- casualty losses, and
- equipment rental.

You should also have one final category called "miscellaneous" for occasional expenses that don't fit any existing category. However, don't use a miscellaneous category on your Schedule E—it's not allowed. You must have a descriptive category for each expense; you can't claim an expense as miscellaneous. Don't list your depreciation expenses in your expense journal. These belong in your separate asset records. You won't need a category for your car expenses unless you use the actual expense method to figure your deduction.

Now, sit down with your bills and receipts and sort them into categorized piles to determine which categories you need in your expense journal. In separate columns, list the date, amount, and name of the person or company paid for each transaction. If you pay by credit card or check, indicate it in a separate column. Periodically go through your check register, credit card slips, receipts, and other expense records and record the required information for each transaction.

If you own more than one property you rent short-term—for example, you rent both your main home and your vacation home—some of the items you buy will benefit more than just one property. Good examples are tools and office supplies you use for all your properties, or legal, accounting, or other professional services that apply to all your properties. In this event, you'll have to allocate the expense among your properties. The IRS does not require that you use any particular method to do this. But whatever method you use must be reasonable and used consistently. One allocation method is simply to divide the expense involved equally among your properties. This makes sense where the properties generate about the same rental income each year. If your rental properties vary greatly in size, a more reasonable way to allocate expenses is by the gross income they generate.

Rental Income

Of course, you must also keep track of how much money you earn from your rental activity and report it to the IRS on your Schedule E. If you rent your property through Airbnb or another online rental platform that processes your payments for you, your rental income should be recorded in your online account. You can download this information and record it in your income and expense journal. As is the case with expenses, if you rent multiple properties to short-term guests, you must keep separate track of the income you earn for each property.

Supporting Documents for Your Expenses

The IRS requires that you have documents to support the deductions you claim on your tax return. In the absence of a supporting document, an IRS auditor may conclude that an item you claim as a rental activity expense is really a personal expense, or that you never bought the item at all. Either way, your deduction will be disallowed or reduced.

The supporting documents you need depend on the type of deduction. However, at a minimum, every deduction should be supported by documentation showing:

- what you purchased for your rental activity
- how much you paid for it, and
- whom (or what company) you bought it from.

You must meet additional record-keeping requirements for local transportation, travel, meal, and gift deductions, as well as for certain long-term assets that you buy for your rental activity. (These rules are covered below.)

You can meet the basic requirements by keeping the following types of documentation:

- canceled checks
- sales receipts
- account statements
- credit card sales slips
- invoices, and
- petty cash slips for small cash payments (these are preprinted receipts that say you paid in cash; you can get them at any stationery store).

For some types of items that you use for both rental and personal purposes—computers are one example—you might be required to keep careful records of your use. (See "Asset Records," below, for the stricter rules that apply to these types of expenses.)

Using a credit card is a great way to pay rental expenses. The credit card slip will prove that you bought the item listed on the slip. You'll also have a monthly statement to back up your credit card slips.

Sometimes, you'll need to use an account statement to prove an expense. Most banks no longer return canceled checks, or you may pay for something with a debit card or another electronic funds transfer method. Moreover, you may not always have a credit card slip when you pay by credit card—for example, when you buy an item over the Internet. In these situations, the IRS will accept an account statement as proof that you purchased the item. The chart below shows what type of information you need on an account statement.

Proving Payments With Bank Statements	
If payment is by:	**The statement must show:**
Check	Check number; amount; payee's name;
	Date the check amount was posted to the account by the bank
Electronic funds transfer	Amount transferred; payee's name;
	Date the amount transferred was posted to the account by the bank
Credit card	Amount charged; payee's name; transaction date

Asset Records

You need a separate set of records for your long-term assets. These consist primarily of your rental building or buildings, but they also include property such as computers and furniture, appliances you separately depreciate, and real property improvements. Such long-term property is ordinarily depreciated over several years, not deducted in a single year like operating expenses. Depreciation is covered in detail in Chapter 7.

When you purchase any property with a useful life of more than one year, you must keep records to verify:

- when and how you acquired the asset
- the purchase price
- how you used the asset
- the cost of any improvements—for example, adding a new roof to a rental building
- Section 179 deductions taken (see Chapter 7)
- regular and bonus depreciation taken
- when and how you disposed of the asset
- the selling price, and
- expenses of the sale.

You should create a depreciation worksheet showing this information for all your long-term assets, and update it each year. The instructions to IRS Form 4562, *Depreciation and Amortization (Including Information on Listed Property)*, contain a blank worksheet. You can also use a spreadsheet or computer accounting program, such as *QuickBooks*. You don't need to file the worksheet with your tax returns, but it will provide you with all the information you need to claim your depreciation deductions on your taxes. And you will need it if you are audited.

Listed Property

The IRS is especially interested in certain kinds of property that taxpayers can easily use personally—but claim that they purchased for their business. To minimize the chances of abuse, the IRS separates these properties into a list—which is called listed property. Listed property gets extra scrutiny and has special documentation requirements. Listed property includes:

- cars, boats, airplanes, motorcycles, and other vehicles, and
- any other property generally used for entertainment, recreation, or amusement—for example, cameras and camcorders.

Keep an appointment book, logbook, rental diary, or calendar showing the dates, times, and reasons for which the property is used—both for rental and personal purchases. Your mileage log will satisfy this requirement for your car (see below).

Asset Files

You should establish an asset file where you keep all your records supporting your depreciation deductions. This doesn't have to be anything fancy. An accordion file will work fine. Keep your real property closing statements and any documentation showing the cost of the land, such as appraisals and property tax statements.

File your receipts for each long-term asset you purchase, as well as canceled checks or credit card statements proving how much you paid. It's particularly important to keep receipts for real property improvements, because these will affect the tax basis of your real property. (See Chapter 7.)

You need not file any of these supporting documents with your tax returns, but you must have them available in case the IRS audits you and questions your depreciation deductions.

Records Required for Local Travel

If you use a car or another vehicle for your rental activity, you can be entitled to take a deduction for gas and other auto expenses. You can either deduct the actual cost of your gas and other expenses, or take the standard rate deduction based on the number of rental miles you drive. Either way, you must keep a record of:

- your mileage
- the dates of your rental business trips
- the places you drove to for rental business, and
- the rental business purpose for your trips.

The last three items are relatively easy to keep track of. You can record the information in your appointment book, calendar, or day planner. Or, you can record it in a mileage log.

Calculating your mileage takes more work. The IRS wants to know the total number of miles you drove during the year for your rental business, your commuting miles, and your personal driving other than commuting.

To keep track of your rental activity driving, you can use either a paper mileage logbook that you keep in your car or an electronic application. There are dozens of apps that you can use to record your mileage with an iPhone or similar device.

Tracking Rental Mileage

Record your mileage when you use your car for your rental activity. If you record your mileage with an electronic app, check the manual to see how to implement this system. If you use a paper mileage logbook, here's what to do:

- Obtain a mileage logbook and keep it in your car with a pen attached.
- Note your odometer reading in the logbook at the beginning and end of every year that you use the car for rental purposes. (If you don't know your January 1 odometer reading for this year, you might be able to estimate it by looking at auto repair receipts that note your mileage.)
- Record your mileage and note the rental purpose for the trip every time you use your car for rental purposes.
- Add up your rental activity mileage when you get to the end of each page in the logbook (this way, you'll only have to add the page totals at the end of the year instead of all the individual entries).

At the end of the year, your logbook will show the total rental activity miles you drove during the year. Calculate the total miles you drove during the year by subtracting your January 1 odometer reading from your December 31 reading.

If you use the actual expense method, you must also calculate the percentage of your driving for rental use. Do this by dividing your rental miles by your total miles.

Sampling Method

If you drive about the same amount for rental purposes throughout the year you can use the sampling method to track your method. However, if you only rent your property certain times of the year—for example, during the summer—you can't use this method.

With the sampling method you keep track of your rental mileage for a sample portion of the year and use your figures for that period to extrapolate your rental mileage for the whole year. Your sample period must be at least 90 days—for example, the first three months of the year. Alternatively, you may sample one week each month—for example, the first week of every month. You don't have to use the first three months of the year or the first week of every month; you could use any other three month period or the second, third, or fourth week of every month. Use whatever works best for you—you want your sample period to be as representative as possible of the rental travel you do throughout the year.

You must keep track of the total miles you drove during the year by taking odometer readings on January 1 and December 31 and deduct any atypical mileage before applying your sample results.

Keeping Track of Actual Expenses

If you take the deduction for your actual auto expenses instead of using the standard rate (or if you are thinking about switching to this method), keep receipts for all of your auto-related expenses, including gasoline, oil, tires, repairs, and insurance.

Allocating Your Rental Miles

You are required to list on Schedule E your car expenses for each rental property you own. This is no problem if you only own one home you rent to short-term guests. But things can get more complicated if you own more than one, because you may make some trips that benefit more than one property at the same time—for example, a trip to the hardware store to purchase supplies you'll use for all your properties. In this event, you must allocate your mileage among your properties. You can split your mileage equally or use a percentage based on the income your properties earn.

Records for Long-Distance Travel, Meals, and Gifts

Deductions for travel, meals, and gifts are hot button items for the IRS because they have been greatly abused by many taxpayers. You need to have more records for these expenses than for almost any others, and they will be closely scrutinized if you're audited.

Whenever you incur an expense for rental-related travel, meals, or gifts, you must document the following facts:

- **The date.** The date you incurred the expense will usually be listed on a receipt or credit card slip; appointment books, day planners, and similar documents have the dates preprinted on each page, so entries on the appropriate page automatically date the expense.
- **The amount.** You'll need to be able to prove how much you spent, including tax and tip for meals.
- **The place.** Where you incurred the expense will usually be shown on a receipt, or you can record it in an appointment book.
- **The rental activity purpose.** You'll have to be able to show that the expense was incurred for your rental activity—for example, that you took an out-of-town trip to inspect or repair your property.
- **The rental activity relationship.** If gifts are involved, show the business relationship of the people receiving the gift—for example, list their names and any other information needed to establish their relation to you as a host.

The chart below shows the information your records must contain for travel, meal, and gift expenses.

Receipts to Keep	
Type of Expense	**Receipts to Save**
Travel	Airplane, train, or bus ticket stubs; travel agency receipts; rental car; and so on
Meals	Meal check; credit card slip
Lodging	Statement or bill from hotel or other lodging provider; your own written records for cleaning, laundry, telephone charges, tips, and other charges not shown separately on hotel statement
Gifts	Sales receipts, credit card statements, canceled checks

The IRS does not require you to keep receipts, canceled checks, credit card slips, or any other supporting documents for travel, meal, and gift expenses that cost less than $75. *However, you must still document the four facts (five, for gifts) listed above.* This exception does not apply to lodging—that is, hotel or similar costs—when you travel for your rental activity. You do need receipts for these expenses, even if they cost less than $75.

All this record keeping is not as hard as it sounds. You can record the facts you have to document in a variety of ways, and the information doesn't have to be all in one place. Information that is shown on a receipt, canceled check, or another item need not be duplicated in a log, appointment book, calendar, or account book. Thus, for example, you can record the facts with:

- a receipt, credit card slip, or similar document alone
- a receipt combined with an appointment book entry, or
- an appointment book entry alone (for expenses less than $75).

However you document your expense, you are supposed to do it in a timely manner. You don't need to record the details of every expense on the day you incur it. It is sufficient to record them on a weekly basis. However, if you're prone to forget details, it's best to get everything you need in writing within a day or two.

Proof Required for Travel and Gift Deductions	
Type of Expense	**Records must show**
Travel	**Amount.** Cost of each separate expense for travel, lodging, meals. Incidental expenses may be totaled in categories such as taxis, daily meals, and so on.
	Time. Dates you left and returned for each trip, and the number of days spent on business
	Place or Description. Name of city, town, or other destination
	Business Purpose and Relationship. Business purpose for the expense, or the benefit gained or expected to be gained
Gifts	**Amount.** Cost of gift
	Time. Date of gift
	Place or Description. Description of gift
	Business Purpose and Relationship. Same as for travel

Property Usage Record

Finally, you need to have a record of how your home was used throughout the year—that is, how many days it was:

- used personally by you or others
- rented to short-term guests, and
- not in use because it was vacant or undergoing repairs or maintenance.

The rules for determining what constitutes each type of use are covered in detail in Chapter 9. You should keep track of each type of use with a calendar or spreadsheet.

Also, keep track of how many short-term guests you rent to during the year. A good way to prove to the IRS how long your guests—paying and otherwise—stayed in your vacation home is to have them all sign and date a visitors' book. You can create one yourself or buy one from a stationery store. ●

Index